DENTURES:
The Ultimate Guide to Dentures & Denture Care for a Beautifully Restored Smile

Kristen Berube, D.D.

All rights reserved. No part of this publication may be reproduced, stored in a retrieval system or transmitted, in any form, or by any means, electronic, mechanical, recorded, photocopied, or otherwise, without the prior written permission of both the copyright owner and the above publisher of this book, except by a reviewer who may quote brief passages in a review. The scanning, uploading, and distribution of this book via the Internet or via any other means without the permission of the publisher is illegal and punishable by law. Please purchase only authorized electronic editions and do not participate in or encourage electronic piracy of the copyrightable materials. Your support of the author's rights is appreciated. Printed in the United States of America.

All Rights Reserved.

Copyright © 2019 by Kristen Tinervin

ISBN-13: 978-1-7325039-3-9

Disclaimer

We advise that the information contained in this book does not negate personal responsibility on the part of the reader for their own health and safety. It is recommended that individuals follow the individually tailored advice of their dental care provider. The publishers and their respective employees, agents, and authors are not liable for injuries or damage occasioned to any person as a result of reading or following the information in this book.

Cover Photo Shutterstock Photo Credit 492354154
Edited by Blackhorse Business Services
Cover Design by Gecko Designs
Sources: 2020 Angular Cheilitis- https://en.wikipedia.org/wiki/Angular_cheilitis
    2020 Candidiasis-https://en.wikipedia.org/wiki/Candidiasis

CONTENTS

Chapter 1. Introduction-*page 5*

Chapter 2. Denture Terms-Commonly Used Denture Words-*page 8*

Chapter 3. Smile Restoration & Denture Options-*page 24*
- **A. Denture Tooth Options-***page 27*
- **B. Partial Denture Restoration-***page 30*
- **C. Complete Denture Restoration-***page 38*
- **D. Implant Denture Restoration-***page 42*

Chapter 4. What to Expect-Making Your New Smile-*page 47*
- **A. Partial Denture Processes-***page 49*
- **B. Complete Denture Processes-***page 63*
- **C. Implant Denture Processes-***page 72*
- **D. The All-On-4 Process-***page 78*

Chapter 5. What to Expect After Getting Dentures-*page 82*
- **A. Common Questions & Tips-***page 85*
- **B. Adhesive- Friend or Foe?-***page 91*

Chapter 6. How to Take Care of Your Dentures-*page 93*

    A. Denture Cleaning Supplies-*page 95*
    B. The Denture HyGenie Cleaning System-*page 96*
    C. Extra Care- Removable Implant Denture-*page 110*
    D. Extra Care- Fixed Implant Denture/All-On-4-*page 110*

Chapter 7. Denture Maintenance-Living with Dentures-*page 112*

    A. Denture Maintenance-*page 113*
    B. Common Denture Problems-*page 115*
    C. How Long Will My Restoration Last? -*page 124*

Chapter 8. Conclusion-*page 128*

Chapter 1

INTRODUCTION

Shutterstock Photo Credit 769003630

"I have been told I need dentures. What now?"

For whatever reason, whether it be health issues or otherwise, you have been told you need dentures. So, what the heck does that mean? What do you have to do? What are your options? Where do you start? What do you do once you have the dentures? How do you take care of them? I'm sure that you have loads of questions!

This book is simply what I have learned over the 1000's of dentures I have delivered, every provider has different methodologies, but this process has helped thousands of people live their life eating, talking and smiling with confidence. I hope that this denture guide book will help you understand the denture terminology, identify the possible treatment options, help you get used to your new dental prosthesis, and teach you how to take properly care of it, once you have received it.

The more knowledge that you have, the easier your transition from your natural teeth to a denture will be. This book's goal is to make you as comfortable as possible during this process. If you have additional questions, do not be afraid to ask your dental professional; they will be happy to answer your questions to ensure your dental success.

With modern day technologies, there is no reason that you should have to suffer from missing teeth or with painful natural teeth. Living with a great dental prosthesis can enhance your daily life through allowing you to enjoy a healthy diet, free you from painful natural dentition, and by giving you confidence in your smile again.

There really is no reason why you should not take charge of your dental situation and improve your life. Let's get your questions answered and on the road to dental freedom!

Chapter 2

DENTURE TERMINOLOGY

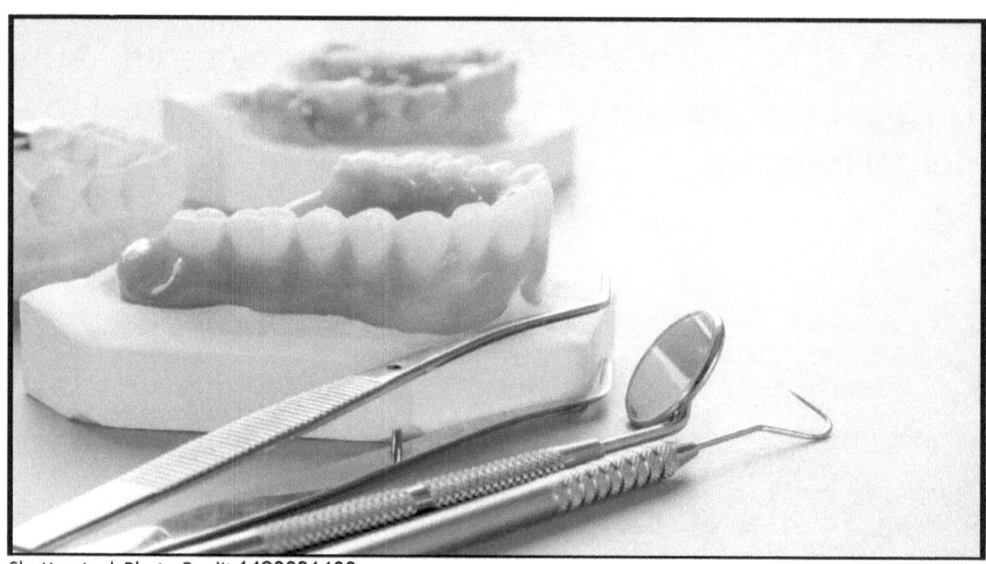

Shutterstock Photo Credit 1420031408

"I would like to understand the treatments I am going to be receiving. Help!"

Here are the most common denture words you will hear throughout your treatment.

Abutment- in an implant treatment, the implant consists of two components.
1- The implant is what the dental provider places into the jaw bone to create a tooth "root"
2- An **abutment** is the part that screws into the implant and is visible above the gums. This is the portion that also attaches to your denture or "bridge"

Aesthetics- in regard to dentures, the opinion of what is attractive or beautiful

Acrylic Partial Denture- an acrylic partial denture is made out of standard dental acrylic, denture teeth, and often times, metal clasps. The use of metal clasps will help the partial stay in your mouth so that you will have limited functionality, such as light chewing. Typically, this is used as a temporary replacement of natural teeth while you wait for a more permanent solution, such as a bridge, a cast metal partial denture or for dental implants to heal.

Adjustment- the procedure your dental provider will complete if you are suffering from sore spots, tooth misalignment, speech problems, gagging, chewing issues, cheek biting, and some aesthetic issues from your new denture

Alginate Impression- an imprint of your mouth, using a dental impression material, alginate, to accurately manufacture your denture utilizing key anatomical landmarks. Depending on the treatment plan, and alginate impression can be used to create a preliminary, diagnostic model or a final model for your prosthetic to be fabricated upon.

All-On-4- an implant supported Fixed Hybrid Denture or an All-On-4 Fixed Bridge, is when dental implants are placed into the jaw bones and then the denture or All-On-4 Bridge/Fixed Hybrid Denture is then screwed to the implants. You will not be able to remove this without a dental provider once they have screwed the prosthetic into your implants. The denture will be stabilized by the implants and will feel just like having your natural dentition back.
This treatment is often called, "A Smile in a Day." With a few pre-surgical appointments to complete a full dental exam and to fabricate your prosthetic, you will be able to complete your new smile in only ONE day. The day you are set to complete your treatment, you will have any

needed extractions completed, implants placed, and your pre-made prosthetic attached to your implants- all in the same day. Also commonly called- *Implant Retained Fixed "Bridge" or Fixed Hybrid Denture*

Angular Cheilitis- inflammation of one or both corners of the mouth. Often itchy, painful, red and can be crusty. Can sometimes be caused by a fungal infection. Contact your dental provider if you think you might be suffering from Angular Cheilitis.

Arch-the term used when referring either to the top jaw or lower jaw bones and tissues, where a prosthetic would be placed

Artificial Teeth- the denture teeth that will be placed into your denture; can be made of various materials (plastic, acrylic, or porcelain). Your dental provider will review the best option for your dental situation

Bite Registration or Jaw Registration Record- a recording of the relationship between your upper and lower jaws. This is used for the proper alignment of your jaws and to produce a proper chewing function.

Bite Rim- an important instrument used by your dental professional to record important information about maxillomandibular (upper and lower) jaw relationship to help them in the proper production of a functional and aesthetic final prothesis. Can be done using a provider's tactile method or with a pin-tracing appliance with bite rims.

Cast Metal Partial Denture- a partial denture that replaces some teeth, and will be used for a more "permanent" treatment. Generally, this type of partial lasts 5-7 years before replacement is required. This partial is made of denture teeth, a cast metal framework and denture acrylic. It is considered the most hygienic and the safest for your existing natural teeth when designed and cared for properly.

Cast Palate- when the portion of the denture that covers the roof of your mouth on an upper denture is made of cast metal. This can be due to the need for additional strength in a denture or the need for a thinner palate in the denture

Clasp- a metal or acrylic "arm" that hooks onto your natural tooth to help your partial denture stay secure

Complete Denture- a type of removable prosthesis used to replace all of the natural teeth, either all of teeth on the top of your mouth or all of the teeth on the bottom of your mouth

Delivery- the appointment that you will get your prosthetic

Dental Examination/Consultation- the first appointment with your dental provider where they will complete a full oral exam to determine the treatments, if any, needed to restore or maintain your oral health

Dental Implant- a screw that is anchored to your bone to serve as the "root" for a new "tooth"

Dental Laboratory- a professional establishment, that employs dental technicians who fabricate the components of prosthetic elements for your dental care provider. (Crowns, Bite-Rims, Dentures, Nightguards, etc.)

Dentition- your teeth, natural or denture teeth

Denture- prosthetic "teeth" made to replace your missing teeth. The denture is supported by the soft and hard tissues of your mouth.

Denture Acrylic- (the pink part of your denture) the material used to act as a base for your denture teeth, sometimes in combination with metal

Denture Adhesive- a substance (can be powder, gel, or pads) used to help maintain a tight fit and increase denture comfort while you are wearing your denture

Denture Base Fracture Repair- replacing a broken area of denture acrylic (the pink part), with new acrylic and sometimes adding metal, to repair the denture from cracks or broken areas

Denture Brush- a denture cleaning tool; similar to a toothbrush, but specifically designed to reach all of the areas inside the denture and around clasping in partials

Denture Ulcer- an area in your mouth that is hurting, generally from a denture rubbing in that area or from recent extractions. Often times, if from your denture requires your dental professional to modify your prothesis if the issue persists. Also called a sore spot or a denture blister.

Extraction- the removal of a natural tooth

Filling- when your dental professional removes the decayed area of a natural tooth and fills the space with another material to save the health of the natural tooth

Final Impression- an imprint of your mouth, once all of the other treatments have been completed, (fillings, extractions, etc.) with a highly detailed material to accurately manufacture your denture upon

Fixed Dental Bridge- an artificial tooth, or several artificial teeth, that is cemented to both sides of your remaining natural teeth of the "toothless space"- creating a "bridge" over the toothless space. When the bridge and the natural teeth the bridge is cemented to are taken care of properly, a fixed bridge can last 7-10 years, sometimes, a lifetime

Fixed Hybrid Denture- Refer to All-On-4

Flipper- a "flipper", is the cheapest way to replace a missing tooth. Frequently a flipper is used for a single tooth, but can be used for 1-3 teeth, if the situation allows. A flipper is a very temporary fix until you can get a more permanent treatment, such as a bridge, a flexible partial denture, a cast metal partial denture or an implant.

Flexible Partial Denture- a partial denture made out of flexible acrylic and not metal. This prosthetic can be used if you do not want metal showing on your partial denture restoration and your oral situation is sufficient. As the name suggests, the acrylic that the partial denture is made out of will actually flex around your natural teeth. Flexible partial dentures often times are more comfortable than an acrylic partial denture, or a cast metal partial due to the less rigid material is it made out of.

Implant Retained Denture:
Fixed- a partial or full denture, secured by implants, that <u>cannot</u> be removed without a dental provider
Removable- a partial or full denture, secured by implants, that <u>can</u> be removed by the patient

Implant Retained Fixed "Bridge"- Refer to All-On-4

Integrate- when the bone grows around the implant and then attaches to the implant surface

Interim Partial Denture- a partial denture that replaces some teeth, and will be used for a "short" window of time until a more permanent treatment is completed. Sometimes used if you are getting extractions completed over a span of time rather than all at once and you do not want to have toothless areas in your smile until the final extractions are complete and a prosthetic is made.
Refer to Acrylic Partial Denture

Mandibular- the lower jaw

Mandibular Reinforcement Bar- a metal bar placed in a lower denture to aid in strengthening the denture base at the weakest spot in a lower denture or when repairing a lower denture break

Maxillary- the upper jaw

Metal Reinforcement- the use of metal wire, mesh or solid metal parts to reinforce a denture. Commonly used when repairing a broken denture or in certain situations where denture acrylic will not be suitable in strength or when denture acrylic is too thick on an upper denture palate (roof of your mouth) in certain situations.

Occlusion- the way your teeth on the top and bottom align to provide you with the proper function (chewing, etc.)

Palate- the roof of your mouth, in denture lingo, usually refers to the part of a denture that covers the roof of your mouth

Post Palatal Seal- PPS- a seal placed in a full upper denture at the junction line between your hard palate and soft palate. This is located at the very back of your denture, to help create a suction seal between the upper denture and the roof of your mouth.

Partial Denture- a prosthesis that restores one or more, but not all of the natural teeth; can be taken out and put back in your mouth at your discretion

Preliminary Impression- an imprint of your mouth that is not super accurate but allows your dental professional to create a treatment plan for you and to make additional customized trays or bite rims that are custom made for your mouth for further appointments in your treatment plan.

Process- the final step in completing your denture where the wax denture is processed, also known as, "transformed", into an acrylic denture that is ready for use through a specific manufacturing protocol.

Prosthesis- replacement of a missing body part by an artificial corresponding part

Oral Candidiasis- a medical condition of the mouth, also known as oral thrush. A yeast/fungal infection of the mucous membranes in your mouth. Can cause a burning sensation, metallic or salty tastes, and white spots in the mouth. Can also appear as a white film throughout your mouth on specific areas. Generally treated with antifungal drugs

Referral- a clear, concise recommendation from one dental or medical professional to another in regard to the treatment suggested and required for an individual patient

Reline-the process of refitting of your denture to your current oral size and condition. Your mouth is <u>constantly</u> and <u>normally</u> changing. Relines are needed as routine maintenance, especially if you have lost weight, changed certain medications or have had other conditions effecting your mouth.

Resorption-the process of your supporting oral bone structure and tissues changing due to ordinary daily forces or denture pressures

Rest Preparation- a small groove placed into a natural tooth by your dental provider to help a cast metal partial denture's retention and to reduce the forces placed on the oral structures from the partial denture

Retention Caps- in an implant treatment, the retention cap is the portion that goes inside the denture or "bridge" and attaches to the abutment. The retention cap is made up of two components:
1. A steel housing, which holds the nylon retention ring
2. The retention ring is made out of nylon and comes in different strengths of denture "hold". Your dental provider will establish with you, the degree of hold you would like depending on factors such as comfort, manual dexterity, etc.

Ridge- the supporting bone and tissue on your upper and lower jaws that will provide the structure for the dentures to be placed upon

Ridge Quality- refers to the amount of bone and tissue that exists in your mouth. The greater amount of healthy bone and tissue that your mouth has, generally, the better fit and retention, your denture will have.

RPD- a removable partial denture- in other words- a partial denture of any kind that the patient can remove without the aid of a dental provider

"Smile in a Day"- Refer to All-On-4

Sore Spot- an area in your mouth that is hurting, generally from a denture rubbing in that area or from recent extractions. Often times, if the spot is from your denture, it will require your dental professional to modify your prosthesis if the issue persists. Also called a denture ulcer or a denture blister. <u>Do NOT try to "fix" your denture yourself!</u>

Soft Liner- this is an option for people who struggle with the fit of their lower denture due to poor "ridge" quality. A soft liner is <u>frequently</u> in a lower denture and will provide a soft, "squishy" liner in it that allows the denture to "grip" to the lower jaw better. This liner can also help reduce sore areas that are caused by denture movement.

Temporary Liner-a thin liner placed inside of your denture to help re-establish the health of irritated gums or to aid in the fit of an immediate denture while extraction sites are healing and changing. Also known as a Tissue Conditioner

Tissue conditioner- Refer to temporary liner

Tooth Repair- re-attaching or replacing a denture tooth that has chipped, broken or fallen out of an existing prosthetic

Tori-bony growths, can be very small or large and can affect the fit of a denture. The removal of tori may be required before dentures are placed because they can prohibit suction from forming between your upper denture and the roof of your mouth. They can cause poor fit and uncomfortable upper and lower dentures, depending on the location of the growths.

Tori Removal- the removal of the bony growths in your mouth that will have an effect on your dental prosthesis. This is usually done at your extraction appointment or at any time if your natural teeth are already missing.

Ultrasonic Cleaner- a machine utilized for dentures that uses high frequency sound waves, which create a powerful cleaning vibration that can reach all surfaces in a denture, including around clasps, denture teeth and into the porosity in acrylic thus; aiding in the prevention of denture staining and the harboring of bad-breath causing bacteria within your denture. An ultrasonic cleaner is a great solution to ensure that your denture gets a thorough cleaning, especially for those with limited manual dexterity.

Wax Try-In or Trial Denture- a trial denture, made out of wax and other temporary materials, but using your actual denture teeth, that you can try in to ensure that you like the denture appearance and the dental professional can verify the jaw relationships, occlusion and aesthetics before converting this wax denture into your final treatment prosthesis

Chapter 3

SMILE RESTORATION & DENTURE TREATMENT OPTIONS

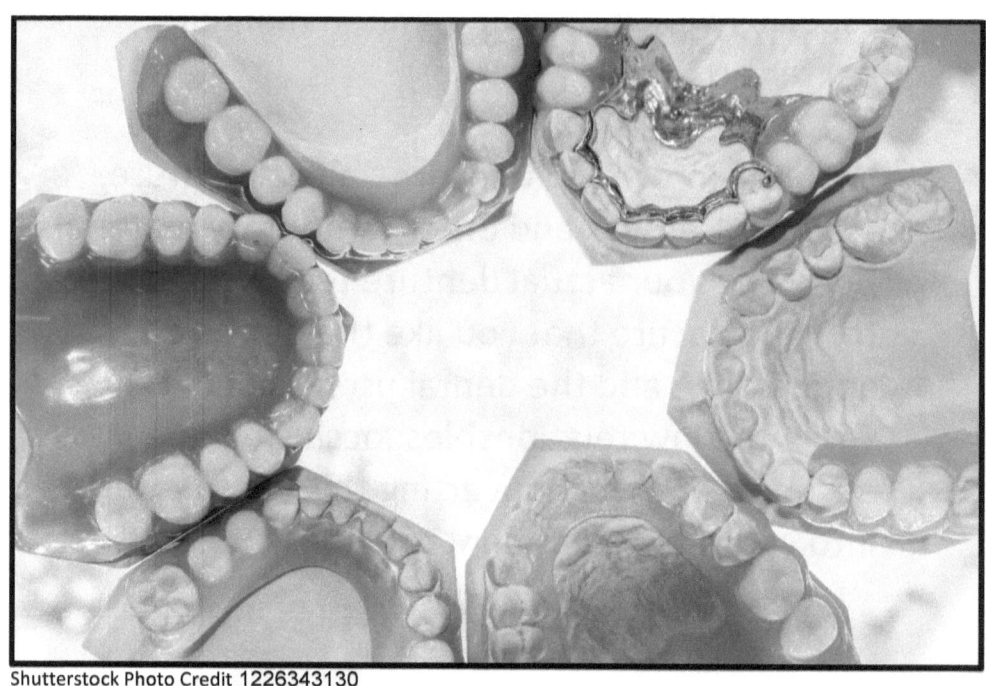

Shutterstock Photo Credit 1226343130

"I would like to know all of the prosthetic options that are available to me before I decide what I am comfortable with."

What treatment options are available when you need to replace natural teeth?

There are several treatment options that vary in price and difficulty. The levels of treatment vary directly with the expense and time required to re-create your smile. This meaning, the more the replacement is like functioning with your natural teeth, the more expensive and the more time it will require. Your dental provider will review the best options for your particular situation, so that you can make the best decision for your treatment.

Typically, dentures are removable, but with more advanced technologies, some prosthetics can be attached to existing teeth or to implants. Implants and bridges tend to be more expensive than standard removable denture treatments and several will require degrees of surgical dentistry. That being said, with the increased expense, comes the fact that your final prosthetic will be closer to having your natural teeth with appearance, chewing ability and functionality.

A key decision that you will make for your new smile is the actual teeth that are used in your prosthetic and there are three main categories of dentures. Partial dentures, complete dentures and implant dentures. Partial dentures are recommended when some, not all, of the natural teeth need to be replaced. Complete dentures are recommended when all of the natural teeth, either on the top or bottom of your mouth, need to be replaced. Implants can be utilized to replace both some or all of your natural teeth.

Denture Tooth Options:

BSDG Photo Credit 2019

A key decision that you will make for your new smile is the actual teeth that are used in your prosthetic. There are several options for denture teeth materials to keep in mind. These also vary in price directly with quality and aesthetics.

Acrylic Denture Teeth-
Single layered acrylic denture teeth are generally the baseline standard of care. While with modern day technology, these teeth look acceptable, especially compared to years back when the standard tooth was very "solid" and looked borderline fake…now manufacturers are able to make these teeth look more real even with one layer of acrylic. The problem with

these single layer acrylic teeth is that while they do look natural, your new smile can look <u>MORE</u> natural and be stronger with a **_Multi-layered Acrylic denture tooth._** The multi-layered tooth usually costs a little more but also will have more coloration depth and variation to help create an extremely natural looking tooth replica. In addition to having additional layers of acrylic that will increase the strength of the tooth; thus, less wear and tear on the denture tooth from everyday use which simply means, the denture will last longer. Providers, 9 out of 10 times, will go with a multi-layered acrylic denture tooth to provide the best product that they can for their patients.

Porcelain Denture Teeth- this is the third option of denture teeth. The denture teeth made of porcelain are very real in appearance and extremely hard, so they last forever and look great. Sounds wonderful right? But as with anything, there are cons to go with the pros of porcelain denture teeth. Firstly, they are made of porcelain, so they chip easily and can also "chatter" if you are using them in a full, upper/lower complete denture set. Secondly, most providers will not allow you to get porcelain denture teeth if you are only getting a partial or a single complete denture (upper OR lower) because the porcelain denture teeth are actually HARDER than your natural teeth and will cause extreme wear on your natural teeth. Porcelain teeth are not highly recommended also if you are going to have acrylic denture teeth on the opposite arch for the same reason. Thirdly, the denture base, the pink part, will often wear out before the porcelain denture teeth, by becoming porous and harboring bacteria which can cause bad breath and other oral conditions. People usually can recognize when it is time to replace their denture because the denture teeth begin to look poorly, but if the teeth appear well, people will put off taking care of their mouth, even though it is very important.

It is important to discuss the type of teeth you will be receiving so that you will be satisfied and well informed on your final product.

Zirconia- This last option is only in regards to you if you are going to be getting All-On-4 treatments and with various other implant situations, another material named Zirconia could be used for your final All-On-4 Fixed Bridge. This material is similar to porcelain in that it is very pleasing to the eye, but it does not chip easily either. These two details make it a great choice for a final fixed bridge.

Partial, Complete, & Implant Dentures:

Partial Denture Restoration:

Partial dentures are used to replace missing teeth when some of your natural teeth are remaining. Partial dentures are used to replace natural teeth that are missing from different areas in your mouth, not necessarily all in a line, but staying on either the top or bottom of your mouth. For example, if you are missing an upper molar on the right side and an upper molar on the left side, a partial can be made for this. These dentures actually "attach" onto your existing natural teeth utilizing clasps. You will be able to place and remove your partial denture yourself using clasps. Clasps can be made out of wire, cast metal or other synthetic materials. Some providers offer tooth colored clasps to blend in with your natural teeth better to avoid the appearance of the metal clasps. You also can get prosthetics that use implants instead of clasping to your natural teeth in order to avoid the sight of metal clasps on your natural teeth.

Often times, partial dentures are given a bad rap in that some say that they can cause harm to your other healthy natural teeth. This can be true, IF the partials are not properly made and both the natural remaining teeth and the partial denture are not taken care of properly to prevent problems. If you do not take proper care of your prosthetic and your natural teeth when wearing a partial, the partial can accumulate plaque and cause additional decay in your natural teeth. The easiest partial option to keep clean is the cast metal partial because the bacteria do not adhere as well to the metal and often the cast metal frameworks are designed to guide the plaque and build-up away from the natural teeth.

Flippers and acrylic partials are made mostly of acrylics, which is porous (meaning it has small, microscopic holes in it) that can harbor bacteria that then will affect your natural teeth and cause bad breath, if they are not thoroughly cleaned. Your dental provider will go over the best treatment option for you.

That being said, properly constructed partial dentures are an excellent option for many people and last for years, with proper maintenance and care, and most importantly, without causing harm. Partial dentures are also a more cost- friendly option than bridges and implants, depending on your financial situation. Depending on the number of extractions that you may require, most often your provider can utilize any partial denture option as an immediate partial denture. If you are concerned about finances, discuss this possibility with your provider but realize that this is not always possible. You still may be required to get a temporary acrylic partial before your final restoration if you do not want to have missing teeth while your mouth heals from extractions if an immediate flexible or cast metal partial cannot be made prior to your extractions. That being said, there are 5 main options to replace some, not all, of your natural teeth.

1. Flipper
2. Fixed Bridge
3. Acrylic Partial Denture
4. Flexible Partial Denture
5. Cast Metal Partial Denture

1. **Flipper-** a flipper is the cheapest way to replace a missing tooth. Typically, a flipper is used for a single tooth, but can be used for 1-3 teeth, if the situation allows. Standard flippers do NOT have clasping to help the prosthetic stay in your mouth. This treatment is just for aesthetics, only, not chewing. Typically, this is a temporary replacement while you wait for a more permanent solution, such as a bridge, a cast metal partial denture, or a dental implant to heal. They also help keep your remaining teeth from shifting.

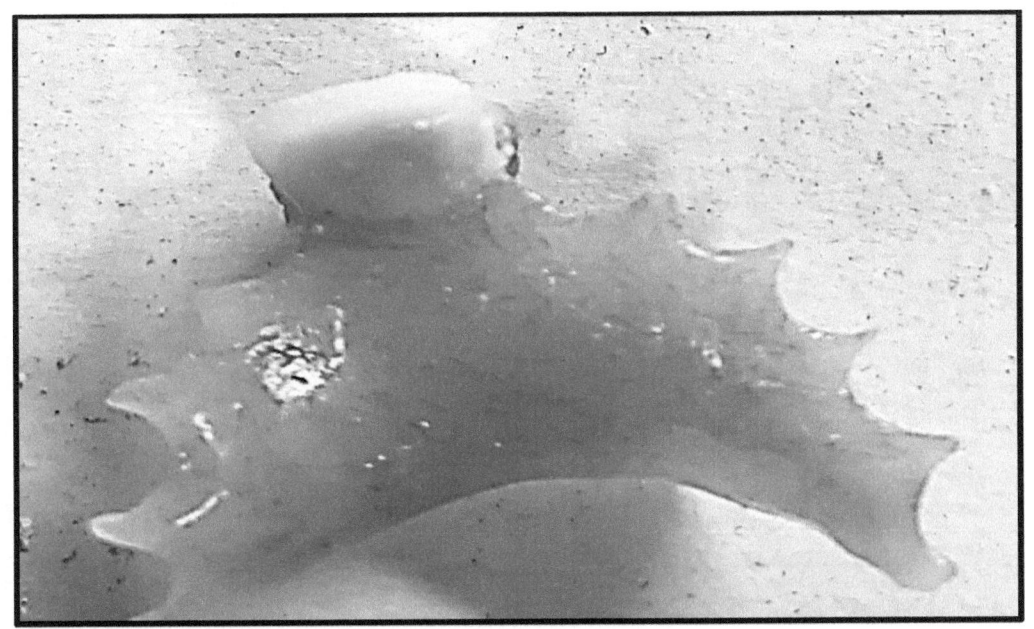

BSDG Photo Credit 2019

2. **Fixed Bridge-** an artificial tooth, or multiple artificial teeth, that are cemented to both sides of the remaining natural teeth adjacent to the "toothless space"- creating a "bridge" over the toothless space. You can also get implant-retained fixed bridges, which will require implant placement. When the bridge and the natural teeth that the bridge is cemented to are taken care of properly, a fixed bridge can last 7-10 years, sometimes, a lifetime. *This is not considered a denture.*

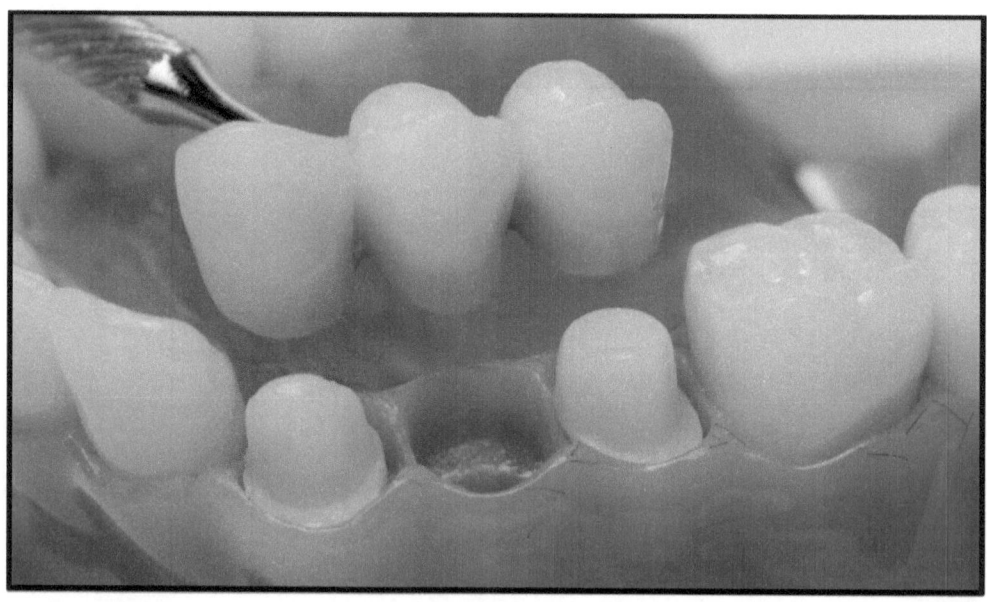

Shutterstock Photo Credit 25133572

3. **Acrylic Removable Partial Denture/Interim Removable Partial Denture-** an acrylic removable partial denture is typically a more affordable option to replace several teeth temporarily until a more permanent treatment can be established, such as a bridge, a flexible partial denture, a cast metal partial denture, or for a dental implant to heal. This option can utilize metal clasps to help the partial stay in your mouth so that you will have some functionality, such as light chewing. Frequently interim (temporary) dentures are used to avoid the appearance of missing teeth if you are having extractions done over time, but do not want to have missing teeth in your smile until your extractions are completed and a final denture can be fabricated. This denture choice is ideal for transitioning because teeth can be added to the denture as the extractions are completed. They also help keep your remaining teeth from moving. Shutterstock Photo Credit 65173732

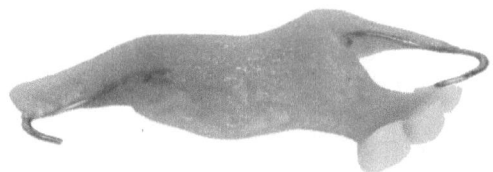

4. **Flexible Removable Partial Denture-** a partial denture that is made from flexible acrylic and no metal. Can be used if you do not want metal showing in your partial denture restoration if your dental situation is sufficient. They also help keep your remaining teeth from moving.

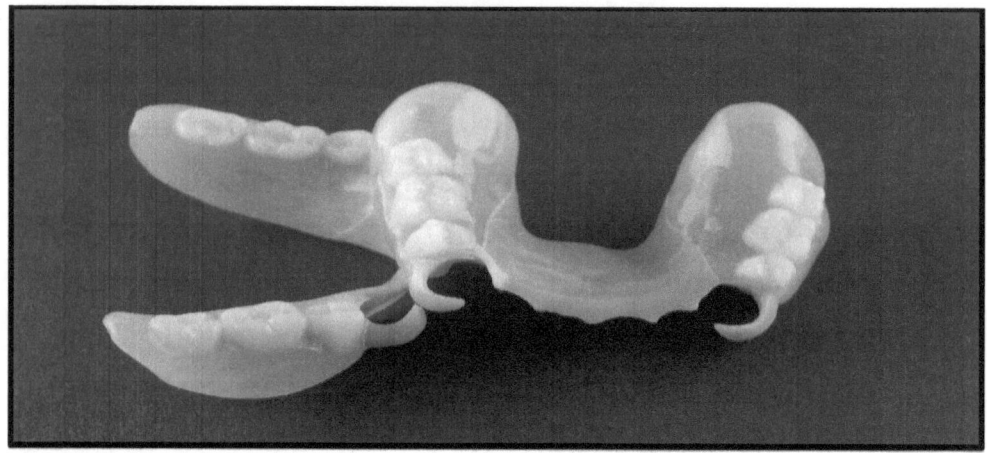

Shutterstock Photo Credit 1375803749

5. **Cast Metal Framework Removable Partial Denture-** a partial denture that replaces some teeth and will be used for a more "permanent" treatment. This partial is made of denture teeth, a cast metal framework and denture acrylic. It is considered the most hygiene and safest for your existing natural teeth when designed and cared for properly. They also help keep your remaining teeth from moving. Generally, with proper care and maintenance, this type of partial can last 5-7 years before replacement is required.

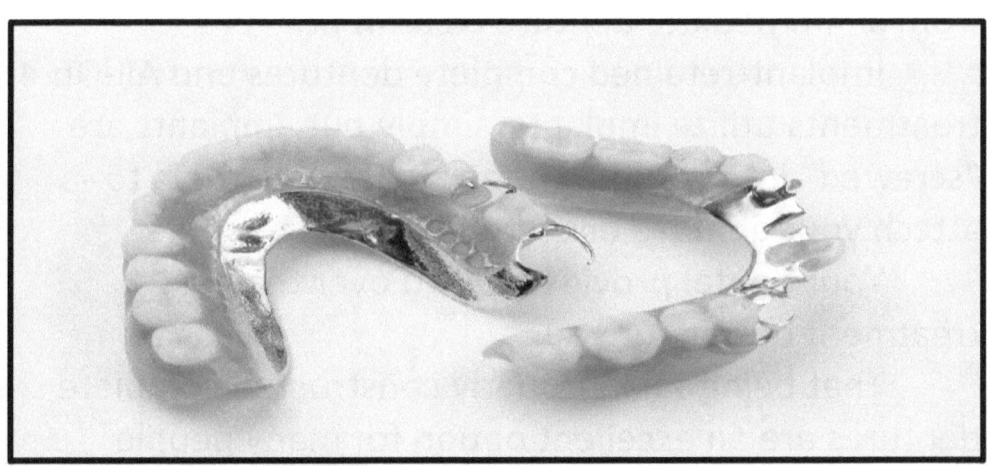

Shutterstock Photo Credit: 1159878529

Complete Denture Restoration:

Complete dentures are used to replace missing teeth when all of your natural teeth are missing on either the upper jaw, the lower jaw or both. Complete immediate dentures are dentures that can be made before you have your teeth extracted so that your dental provider can place them in your mouth immediately after your extractions. This means you never have to go without teeth!

Complete replacement dentures are for those who have already had complete dentures for some amount of time and are simply getting new dentures to replace their old ones or a new set after healing from an immediate denture treatment.

Implant-retained complete dentures and All-On-4 treatments utilize implants, simply put, implants are "screwed" into your jaw bone to simulate roots to attach your denture or teeth to.

Your dental provider will go over the best treatment option for you.

That being said, properly constructed complete dentures are an excellent option for many people which can last for years with proper maintenance and care. There are 3 main options when replacing all of your natural teeth.

1. **Complete Removable Denture**
2. **Complete Immediate Removable Denture**
3. **Implant Denture**

1. **Complete Removeable Denture-** a full removable denture can consist of either a full set of teeth for the upper jaw, the lower jaw or both. This treatment option is used when all of the natural teeth are missing for over 6-12 months. When taken care of properly, complete removable dentures can last from 5-10 years.

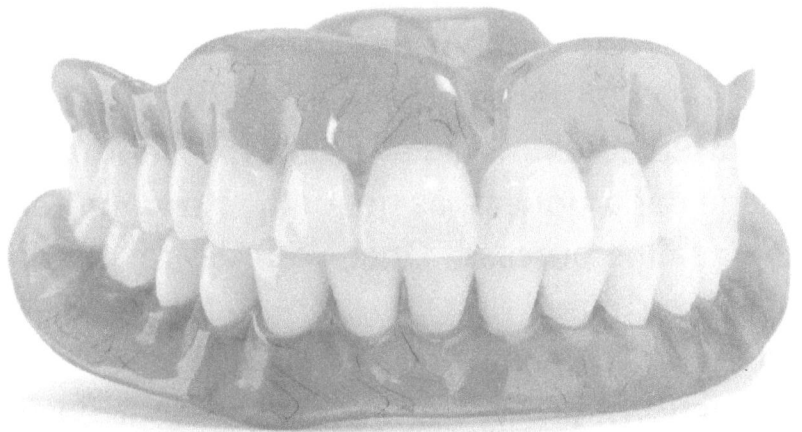

Shutterstock Photo Credit 1055611979

2. **Complete Immediate (Temporary) Removeable Denture-** a complete immediate removable denture can consist of either a full set of teeth for the upper jaw, the lower jaw or both. This treatment option is used when all of the natural teeth are going to be extracted or have been extracted recently, within the last 6-12 months. This denture option, allows you to have teeth made before the extractions are done, so that you never go without teeth. While your mouth is healing your dental provider will complete any required adjustments and refit the denture using tissue conditioners, as needed, to accommodate the healing process. Once your dental provider has determined that your mouth is healed adequately, usually 6-12 months after extractions, you will either get your current immediate denture permanently refitted with a reline if you like the function and appearance of the denture or you will have a new denture made to fit your healed mouth. If you decide to keep your first immediate denture, it can last 2-5 years with proper care and maintenance.

Ideally, a 2nd denture to be fabricated is the best option because once your mouth is healed, the dental laboratory has more space to create the smile appearance that you desire without being hindered by the jaw bone structure that were supporting your natural teeth. The empty spaces where a natural tooth was, will ultimately shrink and heal with time giving your provider more space to replace the teeth and provide a better aesthetic and functioning prosthetic. While the first immediate denture serves its purpose, aiding in the healing of your extraction sites, providing you a smile while you heal and allowing chewing function, a secondary "permanent" complete denture allows for a much better final product in terms of aesthetics, function and fit. When taken care of properly, a secondary "permanent" complete removable denture can last from 5-10 years.

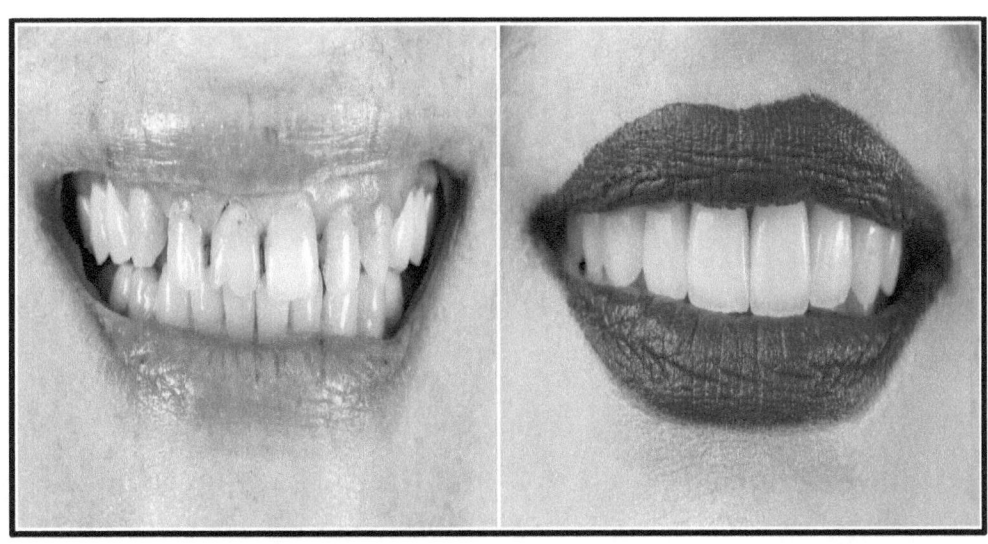

Shutterstock Photo Credit 1445940392

3. **Implant Denture Restoration:**

If you are looking for the finest dental restoration, with most natural functionality and appearance in your tooth replacement options, then you are going to want to consider implants.

Implant dentures can be used in most cases with today's technology. If you are interested in utilizing implants in your treatment, your dental provider will complete a full evaluation to ensure that your oral situation is a good fit for implant therapy. For example, if you did not have adequate bone support available in the area required, you would not want to spend the additional money that implants require, just to have the treatment fail.

Implants- dental implants are when a "screw" (implant) that is anchored to your bone will serve as the "root" for a new "tooth". Over time the bone and the metal implant will integrate to create a "bone to implant connection". Certain categories of dental implants can have dentures immediately attached to them at surgery, as in a "All-On-4" type treatment. There are different categories of implants that can be required to heal for a specific time frame, typically 4-6 months before a denture can be attached to them.

Implant Supported Removable Denture or Overdenture-an implant supported removable denture is when dental implants are placed into the jaw bones and then the denture is attached, but can be taken in and out, at will. This allows the denture to be stabilized by the implants, but you can take it out if you need to. This is especially helpful for the maintenance of the denture. There are several levels of retention caps, a fancy way of saying, there are several choices in the degree of "hold" you would like. This being said, you can work with your provider to choose which level you would like for your comfort and your manual dexterity.

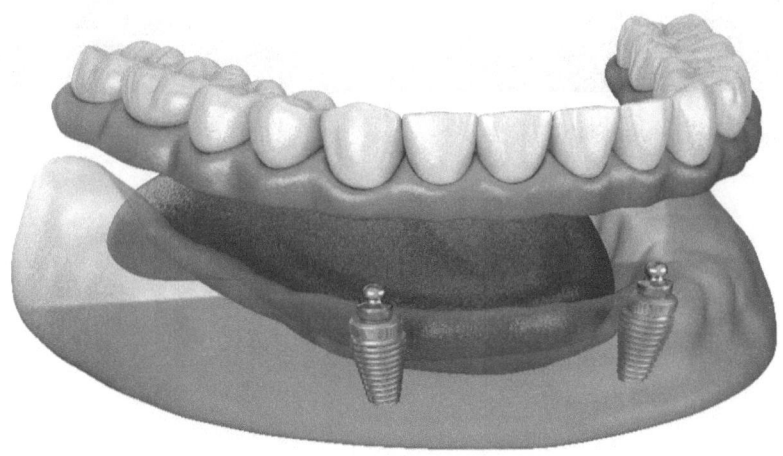

Shutterstock Photo Credit 1426462496

Implant Supported Fixed Denture- an implant supported denture is when dental implants are placed into the jaw bones and then the denture is then screwed to the implants. This allows the denture to be stabilized by the implants and not be taken out, unless by your dental provider.

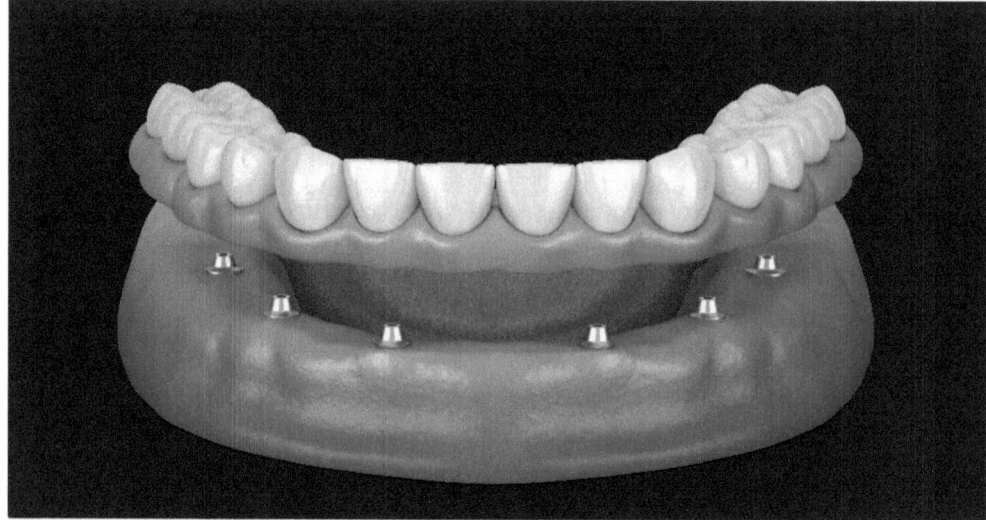

Shutterstock Photo Credit: 1457528447

All-On-4-

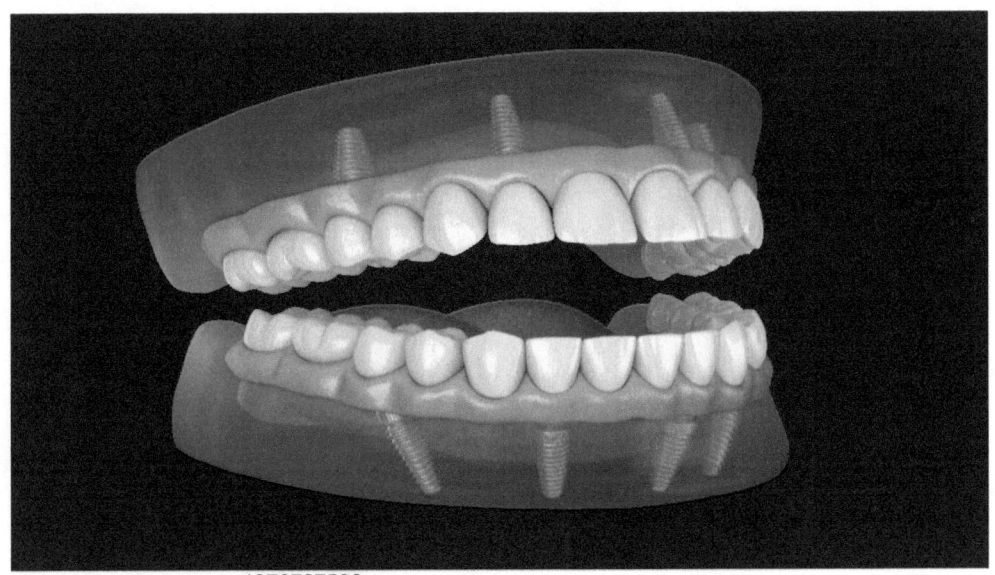

Shutterstock Photo Credit 1376727590

In this treatment option you will have implants placed and the dental provider will immediately screw an All-On-4 Fixed Acrylic Bridge onto the implants the same day. This can happen at the same time that your teeth are extracted or even after you have not had your natural teeth for an extended time period. The temporary All-On-4 Fixed Acrylic Bridge is meant to last only through your healing process and if you have an existing denture the dental provider can sometimes modify your existing denture to become the temporary All-On-4 Fixed Acrylic Bridge in this procedure. At the time that your dental provider determines that your mouth is adequately healed and that your implants are integrated (healed/secure), you will then convert your acrylic dental appliance to a more permanent All-On-4

Fixed Acrylic Bridge which typically consists of much stronger materials. The stronger materials are provider specific for your final All-On-4 Fixed Acrylic Bridge, currently the most common materials are titanium and zirconia.

Chapter 4

WHAT TO EXPECT-MAKING YOUR NEW SMILE

Shutterstock Photo Credit 70482988

"I am ready to start living a happier, healthier life. How do I start?"

The decision to restore your smile with dentures requires several appointments with your dental provider.

<u>For all treatment types, you will begin with a consultation.</u> You will need to schedule an appointment with your dental provider for a consultation. Your mouth will get a thorough exam and then you can review the options that will work for your dental and financial situation.

If your dental exam exposes any dental cavities, these cavities will need to be remedied prior to your next denture fitting appointment.

If your dental treatment plan requires the extraction of any teeth or implants, there are generally four ways to proceed with dentures. The treatment plan varies depending on the number of teeth that need to be extracted and if any natural dentition will be remaining. You will either be getting immediate or temporary dentures, a removable implant denture, a fixed-implant retained denture, a flipper, an acrylic partial, a cast- metal partial, or a flexible partial.

If your dental exam does NOT require the extraction of any teeth or implants, there are generally four options to proceed with dentures. You will either be getting complete or replacement dentures, a flipper, a cast-metal partial, or a flexible partial.

Making Your New Smile

Partial Denture Processes:

Flipper-

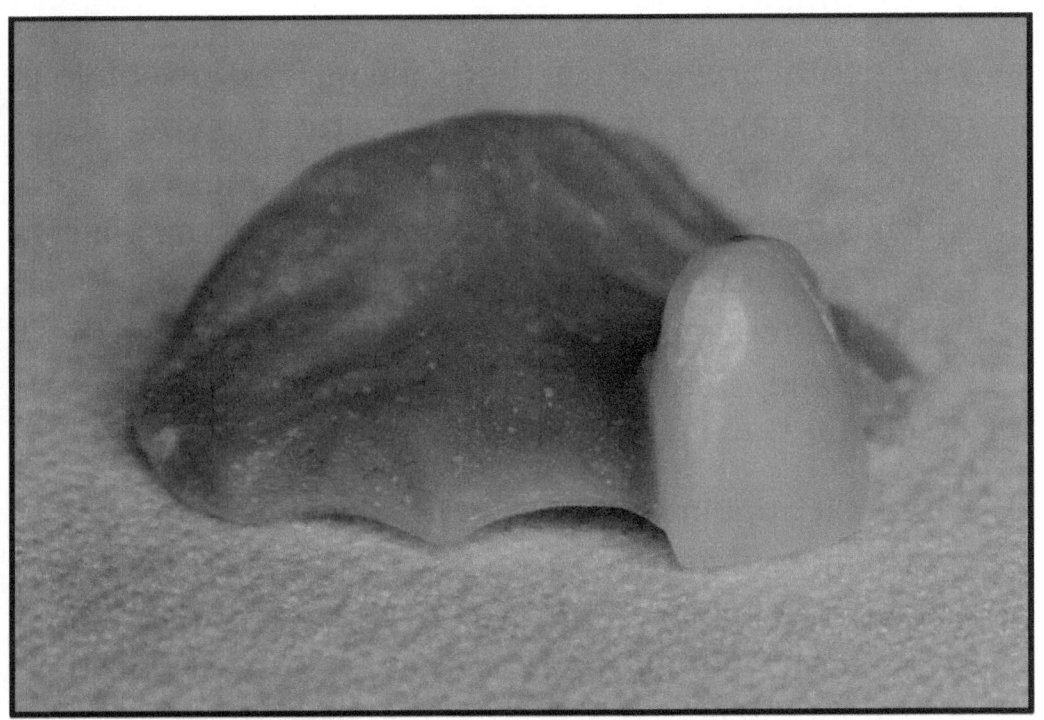

Shutterstock Photo Credit 1583290921

A flipper is made out of acrylic and denture teeth and is meant to be a <u>very temporary</u> treatment until a more permanent solution is completed. Patients often opt for a flipper when they do not want to go without a tooth after a natural tooth loss until a more permanent treatment is completed or if financially that is all they are able to support. You can opt to have small, metal clasps added for additional costs, that will enhance the security of the flipper in your mouth.

If your dental exam exposed any dental cavities or required extractions, these issues will need to be remedied prior to your next denture fitting appointment.

Your dental provider will then take impressions of your mouth to make a model of the structures in your mouth. A bite registration will then be completed, which is basically your provider articulating the angles at which your jaws come together to chew and function. You and your provider will then choose the tooth shape, size, and color to match your natural teeth that the flipper will be next to.

Your next appointment will generally be the delivery of your flipper (if getting extractions and the flipper placed) or a wax try-in. A wax try-in will consist of the actual teeth that will be in your new denture, but they are set into wax to ensure that you like the way that they look and your provider can verify your bite registration, tooth selection and functionality. The fit of the wax try-in will not be as accurate as your final denture.

If the wax try-in appointment goes well, and no changes are required, the next appointment will be the delivery of your dentures to you. If there are changes, your next appointment will be another wax try-in and then the delivery after you and the practitioner are satisfied with the wax-try in.

Once your flipper is made, your practitioner will place it in your mouth and verify the fit, your bite registration and aesthetics. You will then be asked to wear the flipper until your follow up appointment, at which, any adjustments can be made. It is very normal to experience some discomfort or minor issues during this period. <u>Keep in mind, that flippers are meant to be temporary and will not have an ideal fit or function.</u> Flippers can break easily and are **NOT** recommended to eat with. Depending on the location in your mouth, you can sometimes opt to have small, metal clasps added for additional costs, that will enhance the security of the flipper in your mouth, but this appliance is still not recommended to eat with. To aid in the fit of a flipper, many providers recommend placing a pea-sized amount of gel denture adhesive on the tissue-side (the side that touches your gums) and then placing the flipper in your mouth.

Make sure to contact your provider and keep all of your follow-up appointments. **Do not attempt to adjust yourself! Flippers are tightly contoured around your natural teeth for the utmost stability, if you adjust this contour, most likely, your flipper will no longer stay in your mouth AT ALL and will usually need replaced. Contact your provider for assistance.**

If you are going to continue with a more permanent partial, bridge or an implant treatment plan to replace your tooth then you will set these appointments up now in the predetermined manner that you and your provider have agreed upon based on your specific treatment plan.

FYI: Insurance companies usually will pay their percentage of either your temporary treatment or your final treatment, but usually not both. It is usually wise to pay for your flipper out of pocket and then submit your final, more expensive treatment, to your insurance company to get the best coverage.

Acrylic Partial-

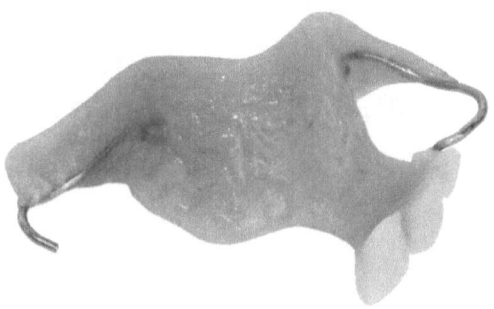

Shutterstock Photo Credit 65173732

An acrylic partial is made out of acrylic, denture teeth and usually has some metal clasps to help it stay attached to your natural teeth to enhance the security of the partial denture. Acrylic partials are meant to be a temporary treatment until a more permanent solution is completed such as a cast metal partial denture, a bridge, a complete denture or an implant treatment. Patients often opt for an acrylic partial when they do not want to go without several missing teeth after the natural teeth have been lost or during the healing time after extractions, until a more permanent treatment is completed or if financially that is all they are able to support.

If your dental exam exposed any dental cavities or required extractions, these issues will need to be remedied prior to your next denture fitting appointment. Your provider can sometimes do an extraction at the same time as the delivery of your partial so that you do not have to go without a tooth in the missing natural tooth's space. Acrylic partials are easy to add additional denture teeth to, if you are expected to lose more teeth before moving on to a permanent solution as a more cost-effective method. Once all of the natural teeth that are planned to be removed or fixed are completed, then you may opt for a more permanent solution.

To proceed with this treatment plan, your dental provider will then take impressions of your mouth to make a model of the structures in your mouth. You will then have your bite registration completed, which is basically your provider articulating the angles at which your jaws come together to chew and function. You and your provider will then choose the tooth shape, size, and color to match your natural teeth that the acrylic partial denture will be next to.

Your next appointment will generally be the delivery of your acrylic partial (if getting extractions and the partial placed) or a wax try-in. A wax try-in will consist of the actual teeth that will be in your new denture, but they are set into wax to ensure that you like the way that they look and your provider can verify your bite registration, complete functionality tests and confirm the tooth selection. The fit of the wax try-in will not be as accurate as your final denture.

If the wax try-in appointment goes well, and no changes are required, the next appointment will be the delivery of your acrylic partial denture to you. If there are changes, your next appointment will be another wax try-in generally and then the delivery after you and the practitioner are satisfied with the wax-try in. The wax try-in is then sent back to the dental laboratory for completion.

Once your dentures are made, your practitioner will place them in your mouth to verify the fit, your bite registration and aesthetics. Your provider can also tighten or loosen the metal clasping to meet your comfort level.   You will then be asked to wear the denture until your follow up appointment, at which time, any adjustments can be made. It is very normal to experience some discomfort or minor issues during this period. Keep in mind, that acrylic partials are meant to be semi-temporary and are not highly recommended to eat with, with the exception of soft foods. Start SLOW!

Make sure to contact your provider and keep all of your follow-up appointments. **Do not attempt to adjust yourself! Acrylic partial dentures are tightly**

contoured around your natural teeth for the utmost stability, if you adjust this contour, most likely, your acrylic partial will no longer adequately stay in your mouth and cause costly repairs. Contact your provider if you need your partial adjusted!

If you are going to continue with a more permanent partial, bridge or an implant treatment plan to replace your tooth then you will set these appointments up now in the predetermined manner that you and your provider have agreed upon based on your specific treatment plan.

FYI: Insurance companies usually will pay their percentage of either your temporary treatment or your final treatment, but usually not both. It is usually wise to pay for your acrylic partial denture out of pocket and then submit your final, more expensive treatment, to your insurance company to get the best coverage.

Flexible Partial-

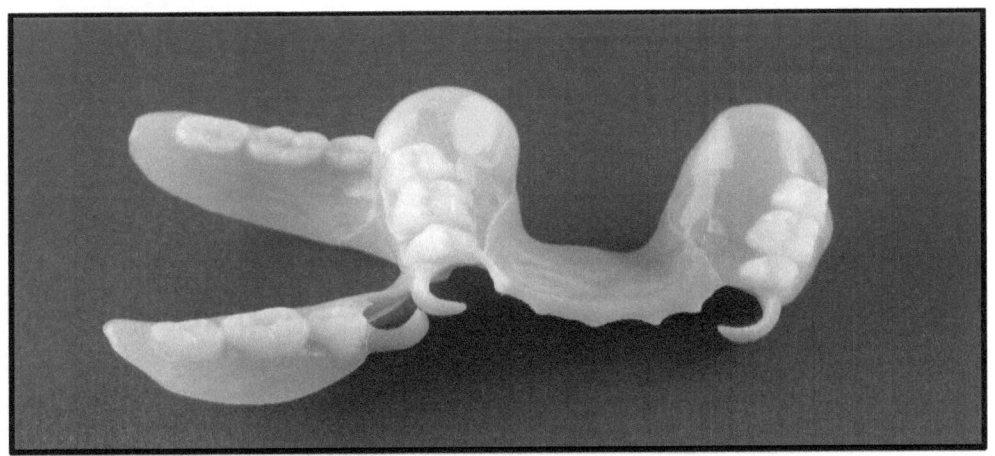

Shutterstock Photo Credit 1375803749

If your dental exam exposed any dental cavities or required extractions, these issues will need to be remedied prior to your next denture fitting appointment. Your provider can sometimes do an extraction at the same time as the delivery of your partial so that you do not have to go without a tooth, as long as the tooth was added into the original design of the partial. Depending on the design of the flexible partial, <u>sometimes, not always,</u> additional teeth can be added after additional extractions but the partial will have to be sent out to a dental laboratory.

Your dental provider will then complete accurate alginate impressions of your mouth to make a model of the structures in your mouth. You will then have your bite registration completed, which is basically your provider articulating the angles at which your jaws come together to chew and function. You and your provider will then choose the tooth shape, size, and color of your new teeth.

Your provider will survey and design a flexible partial denture on your model and a wax try-in will be fabricated.

Your next appointment will generally be a wax try-in. A wax try-in will consist of the actual teeth that will be in your new denture, but they are set into wax to ensure that you like the way that they look and your provider can verify your bite registration, complete functionality tests and confirm the tooth selection. The fit of the wax try-in will not be as accurate as your final denture.

If the wax try-in appointment goes well, and no changes are required, then the next appointment will be the delivery of your flexible partial denture to you. If there are changes, then your next appointment will be another wax try-in. And then the delivery after you and the practitioner are satisfied with the subsequent wax-try in. The wax try-in will be sent to the dental laboratory for completion.

Once your flexible partial denture is made, your practitioner will place it in your mouth and verify the fit, your bite registration and aesthetics. You will then be asked to wear the denture until your follow up appointment, at which, any adjustments can be made. It is very normal to experience some discomfort or minor issues during this period, start SLOW.

Make sure to contact your provider and keep all of your follow-up appointments. **Do not attempt to adjust yourself! The flexible acrylic is very accurately contoured to your mouth. If you modify the flexible acrylic any way, the likelihood of your partial fitting accurately is very low and will be very costly for the dental laboratory to repair the damage. When in doubt, call your provider for assistance!**

Cast Metal Partial-

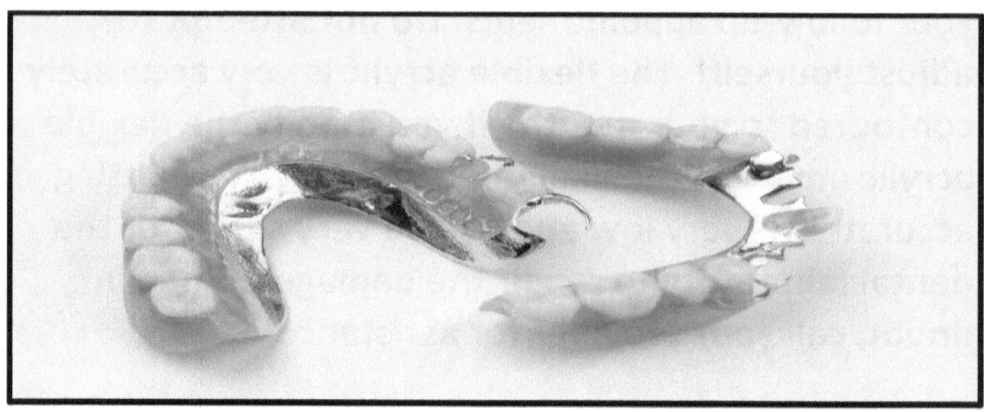

Shutterstock Photo Credit: 1159878529

If your dental exam exposed any dental cavities or required extractions, these issues will need to be remedied prior to your next denture fitting appointment. Your provider can sometimes do an extraction at the same time as the delivery of your partial so that you do not have to go without a tooth, as long as the tooth was added into the original design of the partial. Cast metal partial dentures are not especially easy to add additional teeth to, since the denture teeth are supported by a cast metal framework and a new tooth would not have this structure. Depending on the design of the cast metal partial though, sometimes additional teeth can be added after additional extractions.

Your dental provider will then take preliminary impressions of your mouth to make a model of the structures in your mouth. You will then have your bite registration completed, which is basically your provider articulating the angles at which your jaws come together to chew and function. You and your provider will then choose the tooth shape, size, and color of your new teeth.

Your provider will survey and design a cast metal framework for your denture. Once this design is finalized with your natural dentition, you will make an appointment for your provider to place rest preparations in your teeth. You will then have your final impression taken at this appointment to begin the cast metal framework fabrication.

Your next appointment will generally be a cast metal frame try-in. A cast metal frame try-in will consist of the actual metal framework that will be the main structure of your new partial denture. Your provider will verify the fit, function and aesthetics of the cast metal framework. The denture teeth are set into wax onto the framework to ensure that you like the way that they look and your provider can verify your bite registration and tooth selection. The fit of the wax try-in will not be as accurate as your final denture.

Your next appointment will generally be the delivery of your cast metal partial or a wax try-in. A wax try-in will consist of the actual teeth that will be in your new denture, but they are set into wax to ensure that you like the way that they look and your provider can verify your bite registration, complete functionality tests and confirm the tooth selection.

If the wax try-in appointment goes well, and no changes are required, then the next appointment will be the delivery of your cast metal partial to you. If there are changes, then your next appointment will be another wax try-in generally and then the delivery after you and the practitioner are satisfied with the wax-try in. Once the wax try-in is acceptable, then it will be sent back to the dental lab for completion.

Once your cast metal partials are finished, your practitioner will place them in your mouth and verify the fit, your bite registration, aesthetics and perform functionality tests. Your provider can also tighten or loosen the metal clasping to meet your comfort level. You will then be asked to wear the partial denture until your follow up appointment, at which, any adjustments can be made. It is very normal to experience some discomfort or minor issues during this period, start SLOW.

Make sure to contact your provider and keep all of your follow-up appointments. **Do not attempt to adjust yourself! The metal used in cast metal frameworks is very accurately contoured to your mouth and natural teeth. If you bend this framework in any way, the likelihood of your cast metal partial fitting again is very low. This can cause costly repairs for you. When in doubt, call your provider for assistance!**

Complete Denture Processes:

Complete New or Replacement Dentures-

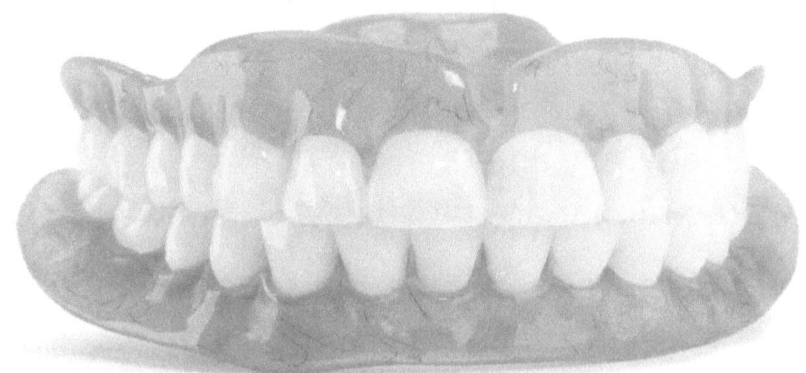

Shutterstock Photo Credit 1055611979

Your dental provider will take impressions of your mouth the make a model of the structures in your mouth. You will then have your bite registration completed, which is basically your provider articulating the angles at which your jaws come together to chew and function. You and your provider will then choose the tooth shape, size, and color of your new teeth.

Your next appointment will generally be the delivery of your dentures or a wax try-in. A wax try-in will consist of the actual teeth that will be in your new denture, but they are set into wax to ensure that you like the way that they look and your provider can verify your bite registration, complete functionality tests and confirm the tooth selection. The fit of the wax try-in will not be as accurate as your final denture and will feel loose and bulky.

If the wax try-in appointment goes well, and no changes are required, then the next appointment will be the delivery of your dentures to you. If there are changes, then your next appointment will be another wax try-in generally and then the delivery after you and the practitioner are satisfied with the wax-try in.

Once your dentures are made, your practitioner will place them in your mouth and verify the fit, your bite registration, aesthetics and perform functionality tests. You will then be asked to wear the denture until your follow up appointment, at which, any adjustments can be made. It is very normal to experience some discomfort or minor issues during this period, start SLOW. Please refer to the section on *Denture Maintenance-Living with Dentures* for common issues.

Make sure to contact your provider and keep all of your follow-up appointments. **Do not attempt to adjust yourself! Complete dentures are tightly contoured to your oral tissues for the utmost stability, if you adjust this contour, most likely, your denture will no longer adequately stay in your mouth and can be costly to repair. Contact your provider if you need your denture adjusted!**

Immediate or Temporary Dentures-

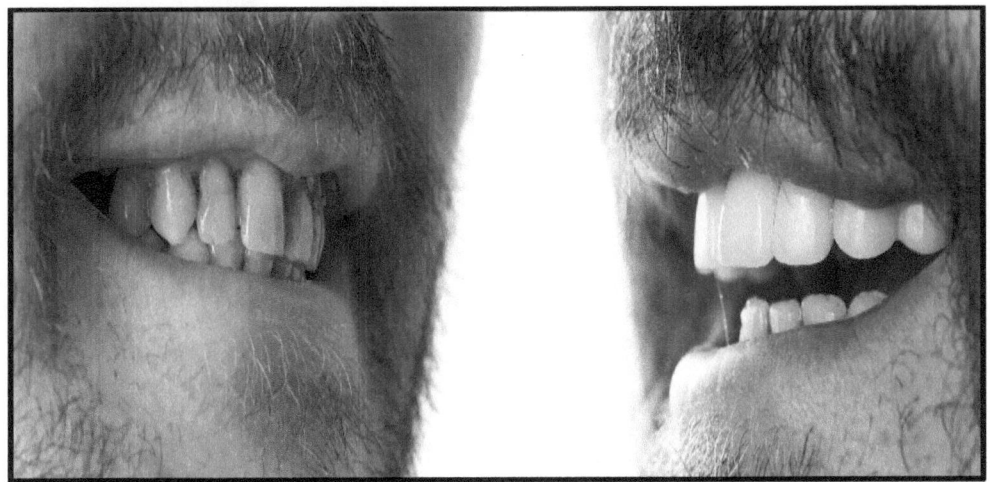

Shutterstock Photo Credit 1009844881

At this point, you have had a complete evaluation and your provider has determined that the remaining natural teeth in your entire mouth or on either your complete upper or lower jaw will be extracted. Your dental provider will take impressions of your mouth to make a model of the structures in your mouth. You will then have your bite registration completed, which is basically your provider articulating the angles at which your jaws come together to chew and function. You and your provider will then choose the tooth shape, size, and color of your new teeth. Given current dental trends, it is not uncommon to choose bleach shade teeth, which are appear like you have natural teeth that are very white. There are many choices of bleach shades and they are very nice looking.

If you are getting your denture made first and then placed into your mouth on the day of your extractions, your provider will not do a wax try-in but will take other vital measurements to ensure the denture product will be satisfactory upon delivery.

Your next appointment will generally be the delivery of your dentures at your extraction appointment. Your provider will complete any required extractions or bone shaping per your treatment plan during these surgical appointments. It is not uncommon to have multiple surgery appointments if you have numerous extractions or in-depth bone shaping. Although, most providers like to accomplish everything in one surgical appointment if possible.

You are asked to keep your immediate dentures in your mouth for the first 24 hours. The denture will help to control the bleeding/swelling, and actually will cause minimal discomfort. The denture in actuality acts as a "band-aid" while staying in your mouth.

Moderate swelling and bruising are to be expected after extractions or oral surgery. To keep the swelling at a minimum and to help with the bleeding, hold an ice pack to the face near the areas of the jaw where teeth have been extracted. The basic sequence for this is 5 minutes of applying the ice, and 15 minutes break. Repeat. Bags of frozen peas work great for this!

You should try and eat soft foods for the first week or two and then gradually determine what you can handle. Dentures are not going to feel the same as your natural teeth did. What you once ate easily may now be very difficult, especially during this healing period.

You will be asked to make a 24-48 hour follow up appointment after your surgery. Please keep this appointment as the provider will ensure your dentures are fitting properly, usually place a temporary liner, and complete an examination to make sure that there are not any signs of infection or unusual bleeding in the surgical areas. <u>Do NOT try to take out this liner or adjust it, as they are very easy to destroy and then will have to be replaced, usually for a fee.</u> If you have discomfort, please contact your provider. The temporary liner will be very helpful to you. It will provide a "cushioning" on the inside of your denture and trust me; you will appreciate it. At this appointment your provider can, to some extent adjust any cosmetic issues, if needed. Once the swelling has resided, your provider will readdress any issues you may have.

For discomfort take the over-the-counter recommended pain reliever or any medication that your provider may prescribe.

Remove the denture 4 or 5 times a day after the first day, and rinse the mouth with warm salt water or with any prescribed antiseptic mouth rinses. Do this for the first week. And you may sleep with the denture in place. After the first 24-hour post operatory appointment, your provider will suggest to you if you should leave the denture in your mouth at night or remove it. This often depends on the number of extractions and the general post-surgical condition of the mouth.

Please contact your provider if you have any sore spots, where the denture is rubbing, so that you can make an appointment to take care of these areas as soon as possible. If you are having problems with speech or a feeling of uncomfortableness, be patient. This usually will pass as you and your mouth get accustomed to dentures, start SLOW. Please refer to the section on *Denture Maintenance-Living with Dentures for common issues.* **Do not attempt to adjust yourself! Complete dentures are tightly contoured to your oral tissues for the utmost stability, if you adjust this contour, most likely, your denture will no longer adequately stay in your mouth and can be costly to repair. Contact your provider if you need your denture adjusted!**

Your next appointment will be approximately 1-2 weeks from your surgical date. At this appointment your provider will assess your denture fit, function, and aesthetics. Your provider may also place another temporary liner to refit your denture and make it more comfortable if needed.

After this point in your treatment, you will contact your provider when your dentures get loose, which is very common, due to the "shrinking" of the gum and bone tissues in your mouth after surgery. You may experience additional sore spots and looseness; this is all part of the healing process. Your provider will have a protocol on how often they would like to place temporary liners to refit the dentures. If you are experiencing pain, please schedule an appointment with your provider to adjust your dentures and assess your surgical areas.

Depending on your treatment plan, after around 6-12 months, if your mouth is properly healed, you will either get your current dentures relined or begin a standard set of dentures. What does this mean?

You have several complete denture options once your mouth is healed. The first, most cost-effective way, is to simply reline the temporary immediate to fit to your new, healed tissues. The second option is to get a new set of dentures made to fit to your new, healed tissues. The third option is to get implants, if you did not get them at your extraction appointment, or the fourth is to get the All-On-4 treatment, commonly called an All-On-4 Fixed Bridge.

There are numerous advantages of replacing your temporary immediate denture.

- Often times the aesthetics are much better in the second set because the bone area is much smaller after healing so what that means is that your provider has more space to place the teeth in better positions for function and appearance without the natural teeth or oral bones inhibiting them.
- Your provider can fabricate a new denture to the new shape and size of your mouth after healing. You will have an appointment called a, "try-in" appointment, where your actual denture teeth will be placed in a custom wax denture so that you can see how they will look and adjust the color or appearance before you get your final prosthesis.
- You will have a new set and can use your other temporary set as a spare.

If your treatment plan is for whatever reason, financially or otherwise, NOT to replace your temporary immediate dentures, you will need an appointment to get your dentures relined. At this appointment your provider will reline, (refit) your entire denture to your newly healed mouth. All of the temporary liner will be removed and you will have your impression taken inside of your current denture to properly refit your denture. After you get your denture back, you will be pleasantly surprised with how much smaller and more comfortable it is. After a reline, it is not uncommon to have a sore spot or two since the denture will be now fitting much tighter. Simply wait a day or two and rinse with warm salt water. You will require an adjustment if the spot does not resolve within a day or two, contact your provider. After this "final" reline, you will then transition to the yearly maintenance portion in the denture care section.

If your treatment plan is to replace your temporary immediate denture with a new denture that will be made to your now healed mouth, then you will begin the denture fabrication process again, but it will be slightly different now that you will not be getting surgery. If you would like to keep your original denture as a spare, you should have it permanently relined at this point also. Please proceed to the **Making Your Dentures- Complete New or Replacement** Dentures section. If you are interested in an implant retained removable denture, please proceed to the **Making Your Dentures- Implant Retained Removable Denture or the Fixed Denture- All-on-4 Section.**

Implant Denture Processes:

Implant Retained REMOVABLE Denture

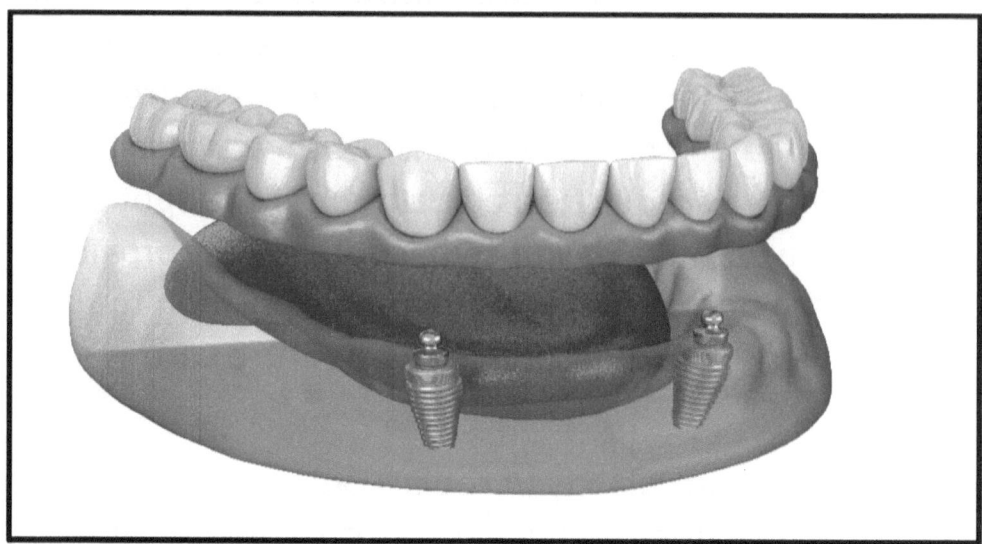

Shutterstock Photo Credit 1426462496

At this point, you have no remaining natural teeth in your entire mouth or on one upper or lower jaw and implants will be placed **OR** you have had a complete evaluation and your provider has determined that the remaining natural teeth in your entire mouth or on one upper or lower jaw will be extracted and implants will be placed.

Your provider will also evaluate the bone position, size, and condition to determine the implant placement location and the number of implants required. Typically, most providers place 2 implants on the lower jaw and 4 implants on the upper jaw, but this can vary depending on your specific situation and your provider's recommendation.

Your dental provider will then complete preliminary impressions of your mouth to make a model of the structures in your mouth. You will then have your bite registration completed, which is basically your provider articulating the angles at which your jaws come together to chew and function. You and your provider will then choose the tooth shape, size, and color of your new teeth.

This denture that has been just made will serve as your temporary denture while your implants heal. You will schedule an appointment with your dental provider to place the implants and complete any extractions, once this denture is ready. If you have an existing denture, it sometimes can be used for this temporary "healing" denture.

After the implants are placed and the temporary denture is adjusted to go over the implants, <u>but not attached to</u> the implant at this time, until the average 4-6-month healing window is complete.

Once the 4-6-month healing window is complete and your dental provider determines that the implants are adequately healed, then your abutments are screwed into the implants and your denture then can be fitted for "clips" or retention rings, to attach to the implants. You will then be able to take your denture in and out of your mouth yourself, but when the denture is in your mouth, it will be securely fastened to the implants, thus alleviating denture movement. Your provider can change the level of retention caps in the denture for a tighter or looser hold, based on your preference. This treatment is one of the best options to feel like you are still chewing with your natural teeth.

Implant Retained FIXED Denture

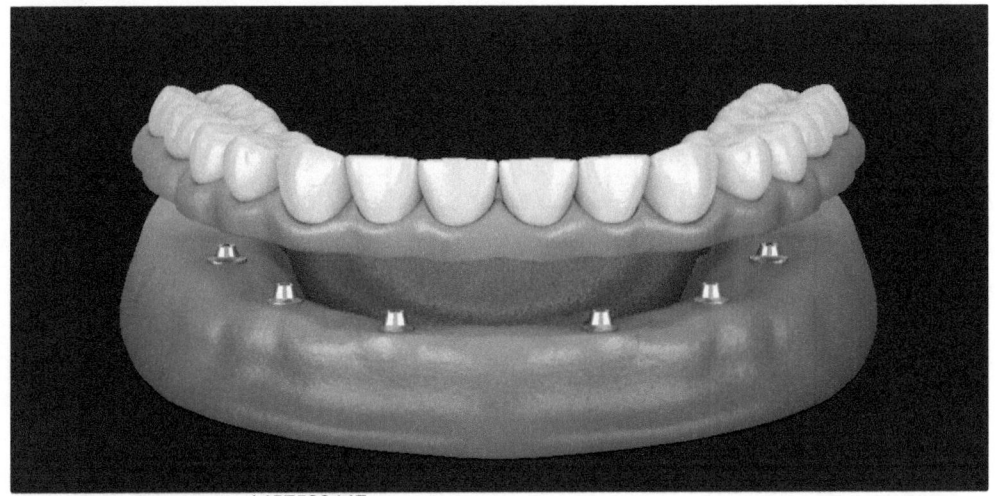

Shutterstock Photo Credit: 1457528447

At this point, you have no remaining natural teeth in your entire mouth or on one upper or lower jaw and implants will be placed **OR** you have had a complete evaluation and your provider has determined that the remaining natural teeth in your entire mouth or on one upper or lower jaw will be extracted and implants will be placed.

Your provider will also evaluate the bone position, size, and condition to determine the implant placement location and the number of implants required. Generally, most providers will place 4-6 implants on the lower jaw and 4-6 implants on the upper jaw. This can vary depending on your oral condition and your provider's recommendation.

Your dental provider will then complete preliminary impressions of your mouth to make a model of the structures in your mouth. You will then have your bite registration taken, which is basically your provider articulating the angles at which your jaws come together to chew and function. You and your provider will then choose the tooth shape, size, and color of your new teeth.

This denture that has been just made will serve as your temporary denture while your implants heal. You will schedule an appointment with your dental provider to place the implants and complete any necessary extractions, once this denture is ready. If you have an existing denture, it sometimes can be used for this temporary "healing" denture.

After the implants are placed and the temporary denture is adjusted to go over the implants, <u>but not attach to</u> the implant at this time, until the average 4-6-month healing window is complete.

Once the 4-6-month healing window is complete and your dental provider determines that the implants are adequately healed, your provider will place the abutments into the denture and screw them into the implant. The screws will be covered with acrylic so that you will not see or feel them. This is now considered a fixed implant denture. <u>You will not be able to take your denture out.</u> If you need to take it out, your dental provider will have to remove the acrylic plug to expose the implant screw and then unscrew the prosthesis to remove it. This treatment is one of the best options to feel like you are still chewing with your natural teeth.

The All-On-4 Process

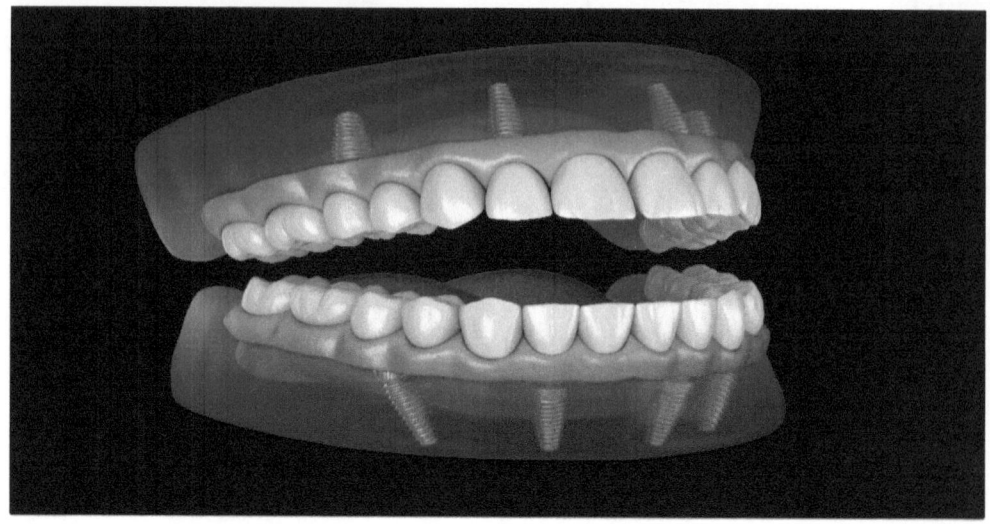

Shutterstock Photo Credit 1376727590

This treatment is generally called, "A Smile in a Day". This is because you will have your extractions (IF NEEDED), implants and the All-On-4 Fixed Acrylic Bridge placement all completed in one surgical day. In order for this to happen, you will have a few steps before you are ready for your surgery day.

First, you will need to schedule an appointment with your dental provider. Your mouth will get a thorough exam and you will most likely be referred to an oral surgeon who specializes in these treatments.

At this point, you have no remaining natural teeth in your entire mouth or on one upper or lower jaw and implants will be placed **OR** you have had a complete evaluation and your provider has determined that the remaining natural teeth in your entire mouth or on one upper or lower jaw will be extracted and implants will be placed along with the attachment of your All-On-4 Fixed Acrylic Bridge .

Your provider will now evaluate the bone position, size, and condition to determine the implant placement. As the treatment name indicates, All-On-4, this treatment generally consists of 4 implants on the upper jaw and 4 implants on the lower jaw, depending on if you are doing both your upper and lower jaws or just one of them.

Your dental provider will then complete preliminary impressions of your mouth to make a model of the structures in your mouth. You will then have your bite registration completed, which is basically your provider articulating the angles at which your jaws come together to chew and function. You and your provider will then choose the tooth shape, size, and color of your new teeth.

After the bone is evaluated for density and quality, an immediate denture is made, this denture will be converted to an All-On-4 Fixed Acrylic Bridge at the time of surgery. This will all occur in the same day at the same surgery.

On the day that you will get your new smile, it will consist of a full day to extract all of your teeth (if not extracted yet), place your implants and then convert the dentures to an All-On-4 Fixed Acrylic Bridge. This is now considered a fixed implant bridge. It is connected to your implants with a screw which is buried inside of the acrylic so it cannot be felt or seen. You will not be able to take your denture out. If you need to take it out, your dental provider will have to remove the acrylic plug to expose the implant screw and then unscrew the prosthesis to remove it.

After approximately 1 year of healing, your temporary acrylic bridge will need to be replaced with a final prosthesis. At this time new impressions, bite registrations, and measurements will be taken. Any changes in the appearance of your temporary that you would like to adjust for your permanent All-On-4 Fixed Acrylic Bridge will be addressed now as well. For example, if you would like whiter teeth, now is the time. The final prosthesis is commonly made of titanium and acrylic or zirconia. Both choices have superior strength and stain resistance compared to the original acrylic bridge. However, this prosthesis is not indestructible and can be broken. After time, they can wear and will need to be replaced.

When you have an implant retained fixed prosthesis your bite force will be restored to a strength that is the same or greater than when you had natural teeth. In this environment, wear and breakage is not uncommon but this treatment is very effective in permanently replacing missing teeth, especially if you do not like the idea of having a removable denture. This treatment is one of the best options to feel like you are still chewing with your natural teeth.

Chapter 5

WHAT TO EXPECT AFTER GETTING DENTURES

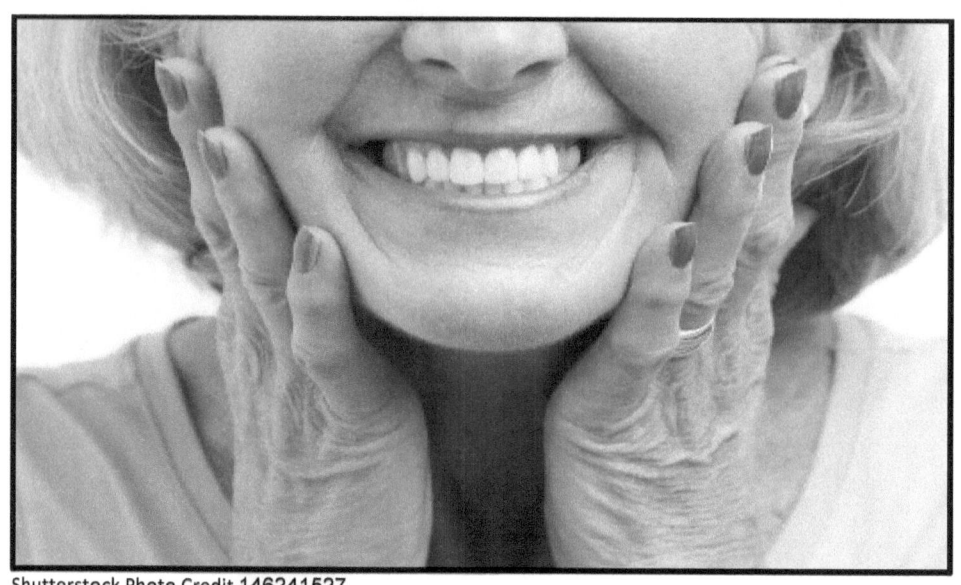

Shutterstock Photo Credit 146241527

"I have my new smile; Now how do I live it with it?"

When you receive your new dentures there are several things to keep in mind when you are adjusting to them. <u>Whether your dentures are your first set or a replacement set, they will still take some getting used to.</u> This all is completely normal and nothing to worry about. Before you know it, you will be back to enjoying everything you were prior to receiving your new smile.

- Start SLOW- do not go eat a steak!!!
- You should wear your dentures for 2-3 nights to let your mouth adjust to them.
- It is normal to have some discomfort for the first few days to weeks following receiving your new dentures.
- If your speech is changed at all by your new dentures, do not be alarmed because this will remedy itself quickly. The tongues ability to pronounce words should adapt after 3-4 weeks. Try reading out loud for a faster adaptation.
- You should try and eat small bites and try and avoid using your front teeth to bite into anything until you feel comfortable with the new denture in place.
- Try and eat soft foods for the first few days and <u>practice chewing with both sides of your mouth</u> to balance the denture and prevent movement.
- Do not be alarmed if your lower denture feels looser than the upper denture. The upper denture has the ability to suction to the roof of

your mouth to increase the stability of the denture. The lower denture basically "floats" on the lower gum surface. Your facial musculature and tongue will adapt to aid the lower denture's stability. Implants are the only way to effectively stabilize a full lower denture.
- Make sure and follow all of your provider's advice based on your specific procedure. Your provider may have additional recovery protocols, especially in regard to implants and All-On-4 practices due to specific implant care.

Common Problems & Tips for New Dentures

How long is the Adjustment Period? Depending on the type of dentures you are getting, the adjustment period can range from a couple of days to up to a year- if you are getting extractions or implants.

Overall Soreness-

Depending on the type of dentures you are receiving, the overall soreness can range from a couple of days to up to a year. Replacement dentures and partial dentures tend to have a shorter period of overall soreness. Immediate dentures or any procedure that requires extractions or surgery will take a longer time period to overcome the overall soreness in your mouth. Your provider will set you up on a temporary liner schedule to help eliminate some of the discomfort you will experience throughout the healing process. If you feel that the overall soreness is not residing, make an appointment with your provider and they can guide you on treatment options to help make you more comfortable.

Sore Spots-

In replacement or partial dentures, sore spots are a more common problem than overall soreness. If a sore spot does not go away after a day or two, you should make an appointment with your provider for them to adjust the denture. Rinsing frequently with warm salt water or an antiseptic rinse throughout the day, especially after eating, will help heal these areas. Immediate dentures will often have sore spots for up to a year due to the changing of the bone and tissue in your mouth caused by the healing process. Often the dentures will become too large/long as the mouth heals and will need to be regularly adjusted, have the temporary liners replaced throughout healing or have the final reline procedure done once your mouth is healed.

Gagging- I feel like my denture is going to make me throw up!

Generally gagging is more an issue with upper dentures. This is because the back of the denture must extend back into the junction between the hard palate and the soft palate (roof of your mouth) in order to create the suction to the roof of your mouth, that will actually hold your upper in place. If you shorten the denture too much, it will no longer suction into your mouth and you may have to use adhesive regularly.

Increased Saliva- I feel like I am Drooling!

Having dentures placed is a big change for your mouth and your salivary glands can go a little crazy. This problem typically fixes itself after a few weeks with a new denture. However, excessive pressure on the salivary duct can make the situation worse. If you feel that this situation is not improving or are experiencing discomfort, schedule an appointment with your dental provider to check the denture borders to ensure that they are not interfering with your salivary ducts.

My Mouth Feels Too Full!

This is a common problem because most people go from only having their natural teeth in their mouth. Now you will have denture teeth, denture acrylic, and sometimes metal. You will get accustomed to this sensation with time. If you feel as though you need additional assistance, schedule an appointment with your provider. In some cases, your provider can reduce certain areas of the denture to aid in this issue.

What Can I Eat?

<u>Whether you are a first-time denture wearer or a denture veteran, when you get a new denture it is wise to eat soft foods for the first couple of weeks.</u> As your mouth gets accustomed to your new dentures you can slowly add in additional foods.

A common mistake that people make is that when they first get their new dentures they immediately go out and eat a large meal, and 9 out of 10 times these patients end up with numerous sore spots and overall soreness. I like to simulate it to getting a new pair of hiking boots. You don't usually get a new pair of hiking boots and go out on a 10-mile hike, you usually wear the new boots for smaller periods of time to get your feet used to the boots and to break in the boots, right? Otherwise, you will have loads of blisters, a couple of sore feet, and I bet you won't be very happy with your new boots. The same methodology applies to new dentures. Start SLOW!

A great way to practice is by chewing Free-Dent, a gum specially made for use with dental restorations, as it won't stick to them.

How do I eat? How can I Possibly Chew with these Dentures?

Getting used to eating with dentures can be tricky. This is a learned skill and, yes, it is difficult at first, but the only way complete dentures (without implants) really will be effective is if you try to divide the food in your mouth between both sides and then <u>chew with both sides at the same time.</u> If you chew only on one side, then the denture will act like a teeter-totter and will pop down the other side of your denture because it acts as one unit.

It is also helpful to cut food into smaller pieces than you previously did with your natural teeth. This will help you get used to chewing with both sides of your denture simultaneously.

Napkins- Beware of Napkins!

So many people, especially with flippers or partial dentures, will take their denture out to eat, place it into a napkin and then forget that they took it out. Then what do they do? They throw the napkin away. Be careful!

Vomiting- Beware of Throwing Up!

If you feel as though you are going to vomit, it is very wise to take your dentures out first if possible. It is very easy to not notice that your denture has fallen into the toilet, bowl, or trash can and then get flushed or thrown away.

Pets- Beware of Your Pets!

Pets, especially dogs, love dentures. Make sure and keep them securely in a box and out of your pets reach when you are not wearing them. Dogs tend to chew the dentures up, mostly beyond repair. This can be a very costly issue.

Speech- Why Am I Talking Like I Have a Bag of Marbles in My Mouth?

Commonly, people have some speech trouble the first few days after getting their new dentures and when the dentures get too loose down the road. If you are getting new dentures, the more you speak, the better. I always suggest that people go home and read out loud to themselves. Your tongue, cheeks and oral muscles have to get used to speaking with dentures, so the more you speak, the faster the muscles will get "trained". In this situation, repetition is your best friend. Keep trying! If you have your dentures for at least 6 months and they feel loose, this can be an indication that you need to have your dentures relined to correct the fit, and therefore correct your speech.

Adhesive- Should I Use Adhesive?

I would suggest using an adhesive, as needed, when you first get your denture. **You may not require it if your denture fits tightly.** Sometimes, adhesive use is more about a sense of security when you first get dentures so that you can build confidence in your speaking and release your fears of the denture coming out of your mouth. See more on adhesive in the next section.

Adhesive- Friend or Foe?

Adhesive can be your friend, but it can also be your enemy. It is very important to use the suggested amount, and to clean the remaining out before reapplying. You can reapply adhesive as needed throughout the day. If you use too much and it seeps out, you will ingest the adhesive, which is not ideal. Most people only need adhesive if they received a flipper or a complete lower denture. Other partial dentures actually have clasps that hook onto the natural remaining teeth and anchor the partial into your mouth. Lower complete dentures tend to require more adhesive than upper dentures because upper dentures can actually suction to the roof of your mouth and lower dentures just rest on the lower jaw bone.

If your denture is not very loose and you attempt to put an excessive amount of adhesive or an adhesive pad in it, most of the time this will cause additional irritation because it will change the fit of the denture, which is very accurately molded to your tissues. Getting the adhesive out of your denture is an age- old issue. Glue doesn't like to come out right? So simply follow the suggestions in the Daily Care Section. Trust me, you will want to know how to do this!

There are a variety of denture adhesives that help prevent food from getting under your dentures and keep your dentures securely fitting in your mouth. It is recommended you utilize a zinc-free denture adhesive to avoid zinc poisoning.

Adhesive Options:

- *Powder Adhesive: used for a light to moderate hold or for general security*
- *Gel Adhesive: used for a moderate to heavy hold*
- *Adhesive Pads: can be used for light to heavy hold, but can also cause denture rocking and sore spots, if not placed properly. Always follow the instructions carefully.*

Chapter 6

HOW TO TAKE CARE OF YOUR DENTURES

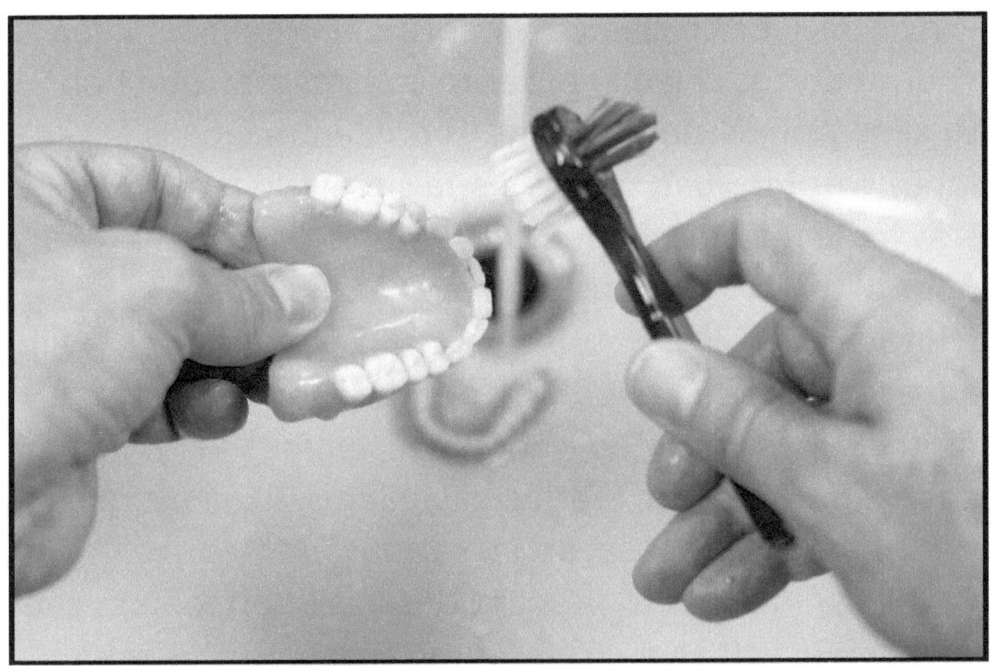

Shutterstock Photo Credit 1555441091

"I love my new smile; How do I take care of it?"

First things first...
If you have any natural teeth remaining- you will need to floss and brush your natural teeth regularly to keep them healthy!

Why do I need to clean my dentures? You must keep your dentures clean in order to control oral infections, to keep oral tissues healthy, to prevent halitosis (a fancy word for bad breath), and simply so that they stay looking good. A denture tooth is similar to a natural tooth in that plaque and calculus (the white/gray/yellow debris that sticks to your teeth) will adhere to the surface of the denture and the denture teeth. This is unhygienic and does not look very appealing. Denture teeth can stain just like natural teeth from coffee, tea, soda, various foods, and smoking. In order to prevent this from happening, you simply must clean your dentures properly. This then allows for less staining of your denture teeth.

So how do I take care of my denture? It is critical that you learn to take care of your new denture in order to keep your smile comfortable and clean.
If you follow a cleaning routine, you will prevent bad breath, plaque build-up, staining and prolong the life of your denture.

Suggested Denture Supplies:
- **Denture Brush**
- **Denture Bath/Box**
- **Denture Cleaner Tablets or Paste**
- **Denture Adhesive**
- **Denture Adhesive Remover Wipes**
- **Denture Adhesive Remover**
- **Ultrasonic Cleaner**
- **Soft Dental Toothbrush-** for natural teeth, gums, and implants
- **Floss-**if you have natural teeth
- **Non-Abrasive Toothpaste-**if you have natural teeth
- **Antiseptic Mouthwash**
- **Oral Irrigation Device,** such as a water flosser -if caring for an All-On-4 prosthetic or fixed bridge/denture
- **Dental floss threader-** if caring for an All-On-4 prosthetic or fixed bridge/denture

---

TIP You can always use dish soap to clean your dentures in a pinch! Do not use toothpaste as it generally contains abrasive materials which will scratch your denture.

Daily Care

I highly recommend using, **The Denture HyGenie Cleaning System ©** if you have **removable** dentures, **not fixed** implant dentures.

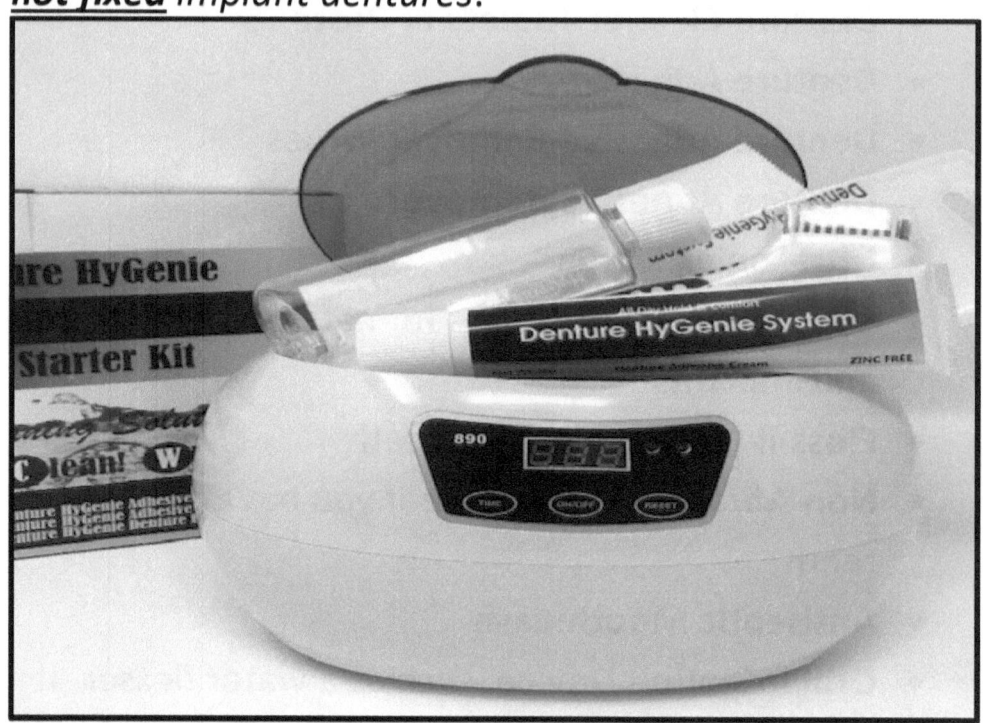

Photo Credit Denture HyGenie 2018

What is the Denture HyGenie Cleaning System©?

The Denture HyGenie Cleaning System© is the ONLY <u>Complete</u> denture cleaning solution!

This is a system that I came up with because, after years of trying to help my patients keep their dentures clean, I discovered that there was no standard protocol, no system on the market and, therefore, it was quite difficult for the average person to have any way to adequately clean and sanitize their denture. The result was that no matter what people did, there denture was accumulating stains, plaque, and causing bad breath. The **Denture HyGenie Cleaning System©** is a complete system that is effective for cleaning and maintaining complete and partial dentures that addresses all of these issues and more.

The Denture HyGenie is the ONLY system on the market that you can trust to take care of your dentures. This system's denture cleaner keeps staining and bad breath at bay by reducing unsightly bio-film and destroying odor-causing bacteria with its tough Stain Vanisher Whitening Tablets. Not only does The Denture HyGenie System keep your smile looking youthful, fresh and white, but it also protects your dental investment by keeping your dentures new for as long as possible. This system can also help you restore your old dentures by getting those stubborn stains off and giving you your smile back. If you struggle with manual dexterity, this system will get your dentures sparkling and fresh without all of the struggle by utilizing the powerful DH Ultrasonic Cleaner and non-slip grip DH Denture Brush. The Denture HyGenie Cleaning System© also tackles one of the LARGEST problems that you, as a denture wearer will face, ADHESIVE REMOVAL. The DH Cleaning System has an effective 2-Step Option to get the sticky adhesive out of your dentures and mouth so that you do not end up ingesting adhesive and are unable to clean your denture because you cannot get the adhesive out. The 2-Step Solution employs a specially formulated, micro-fiber wipe to grip the excess adhesive from your mouth and from the inside of your dentures! Following the removal of the bulk of the adhesive with the DH Adhesive Remover Wipe, the DH Adhesive Remover is put into action by breaking down the remaining adhesive so that it can easily be brushed out of the denture.

Why is this system so Great?
The Denture HyGenie System© is so great, simply because it ACTUALLY WORKS for everyone with complete, immediate, partial and removable implant dentures.

The Denture HyGenie Adhesive Remover, DH Remover Wipes and DH Denture Brush help get rid of the sticky adhesive to actually let the cleaning solution get to the base of the denture and clean it, removes old bacteria-filled adhesive, and keeps you from ingesting any extra adhesive. The Denture HyGenie Ultrasonic Cleaner© Unit and the DH Whitening Tablets, reach into all of the nooks and crannies that are not visible to the naked eye to kill bad-breath causing bacteria and keep unsightly stains away. If you do not have the best manual dexterity, the DH Ultrasonic Cleaner does the cleaning for you so that you do not have to suffer with an unappealing, bad-breath causing denture.

The Denture HyGenie Adhesive Cream© allows you to have a secure, comfortable denture all day long.

The Denture HyGenie Starter Kit© Includes:

- A High Power Ultrasonic Cleaner Unit
- Whitening & Disinfecting Cleaning Tablets
- A Quality Denture Brush
- Denture Adhesive Cream
- Denture Adhesive Remover

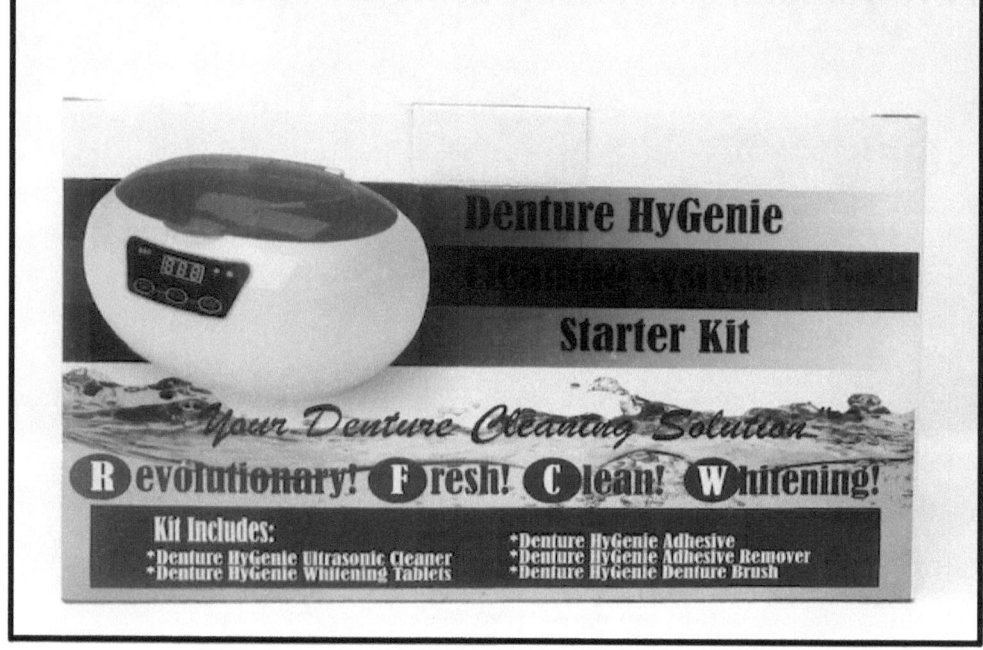

Photo Credit Denture HyGenie 2018

The Denture HyGenie Ultrasonic Cleaner©

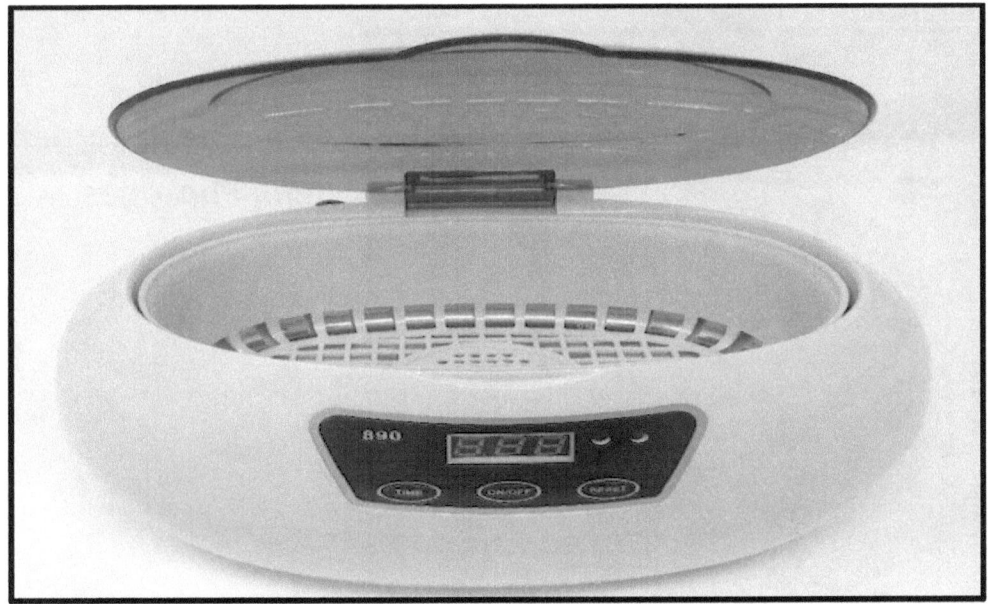

Photo Credit Denture HyGenie 2018

Features:
- Hands-free Denture Cleaning
- Microburst Cleaning Action
- Proven More Effective than Just Brushing Alone
- Comes with a Photo Manual
- Lined with Stainless Steel w/ Removable Plastic Basket
- LED Light
- 18- Timer Settings
- Auto Shut-Off
- For Use On: Complete/Partial Dentures, Mouthguards, Night Guards, Bleach Trays, Retainers, Invisalign Retainers

Whitening & Disinfecting Cleaning Tablets©

Photo Credit Denture HyGenie 2018

Available in Larger Refill Packages

Features:

- Restores dental appliance to their original color
- Use for a cleaner, fresher, brighter dental appliance
- Kills 99.9% of odor-causing bacteria
- Protects from staining and plaque build-up
- 360 Degree Cleaning for fresh breath every day
- Long-standing stains may need extra soaking in the solution

Denture HyGenie Denture Brush©

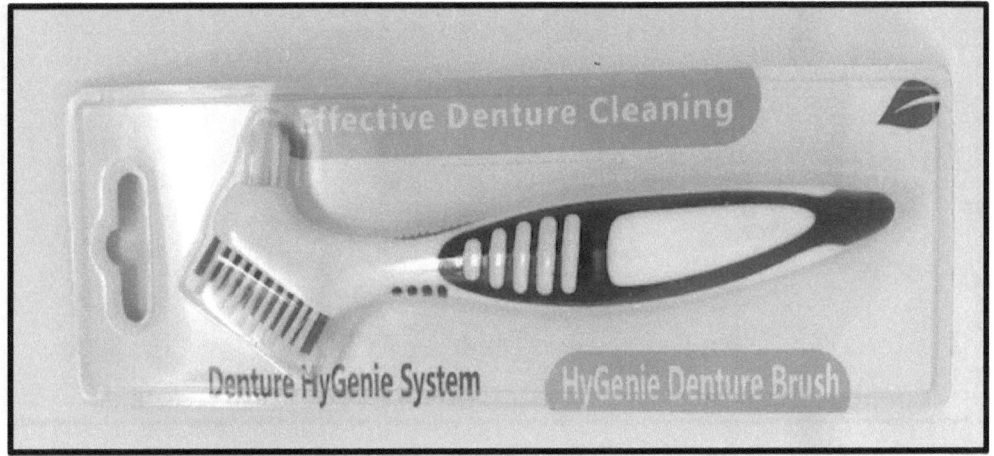

Photo Credit Denture HyGenie 2018

Features:
- A large, multi-tufted brush head helps remove food particles, adhesive and stains
- A smaller, angle-trimmed brush head for hard-to-reach surfaces
- Firm, nylon bristles are strong and resilient
- A large, soft, rubber, non-slip handle provides you easy control

Denture HyGenie Adhesive Cream©

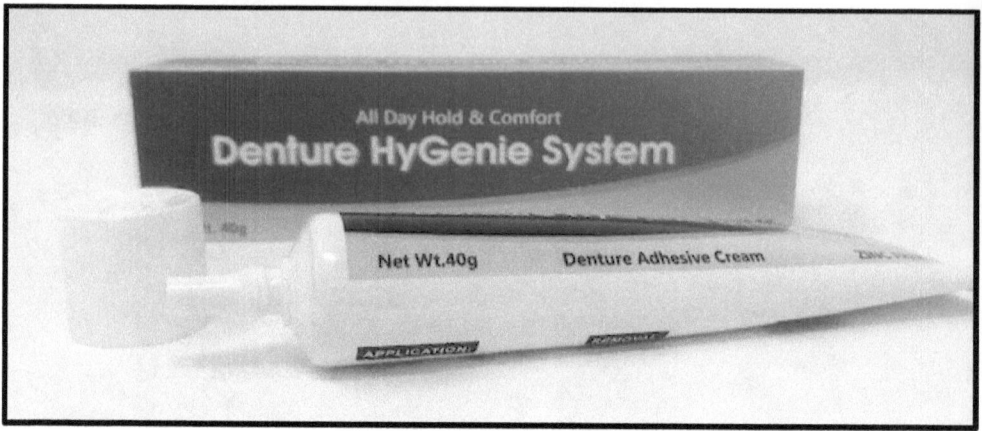

Photo Credit Denture HyGenie 2018

Features:
- All day hold & comfort
- Zinc-FREE
- Provides a sense of security

Denture HyGenie Adhesive Remover©

Available in Larger Refill Packages

Features:

- All natural
- Helps remove stubborn adhesive
- Allows for thorough cleaning
- Helps prevent ingesting excess adhesive

Photo Credit Denture HyGenie 2018

Other Denture HyGenie Products: *Sold Separately*

Photo Credit Denture HyGenie 2018

Denture HyGenie Adhesive Remover Wipes©

Features:
- All natural
- Specially formulated fibers grip adhesive
- Helps remove stubborn adhesive
- Allows for thorough cleaning
- Helps prevent ingesting excess adhesive

How do I use this system to maintain my denture?

1. Remove your dentures with a gentle rocking, side to side, to loosen the adhesive. Try to always handle your denture over a soft surface, such as a towel, so that if you drop it, the denture will hopefully, not be damaged.
2. Rinse your denture with very warm water, NOT HOT since dentures can warp with extreme heat, and use the DH Adhesive Remover Wipes to remove the majority of the adhesive with a wiping motion.

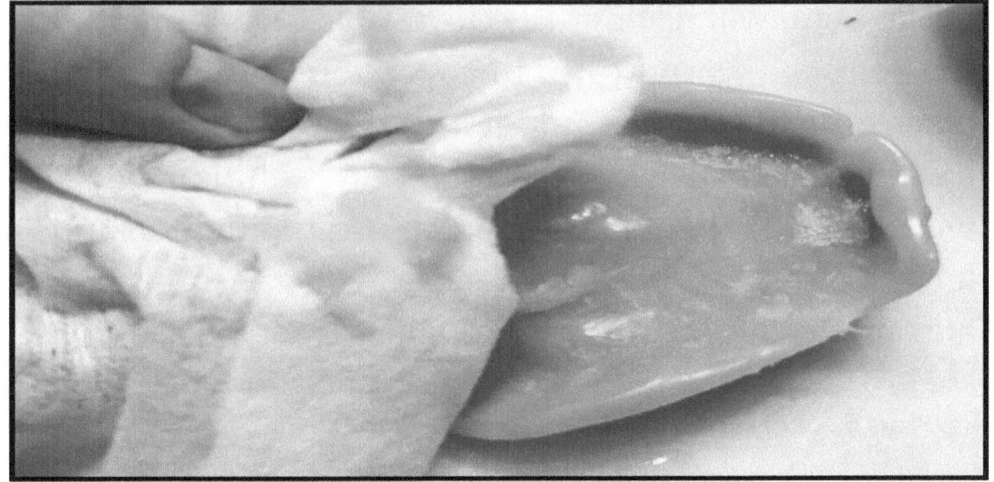

Photo Credit Denture HyGenie 2018

3. Then coat the inside of your denture with the DH Adhesive Remover. Let sit for 2-3 minutes. Use your DH Denture Brush and warm water on both the inside and outside surfaces of your denture. Repeat as needed to remove all particles and adhesive.

Photo Credit Denture HyGenie 2018

4. Next you will fill your DH Ultrasonic Cleaner unit with enough warm water to cover your denture and place a DH Whitening Tablet into the water. Place your dental appliance into the effervescing solution, which will change from blue to clear.   Turn the unit on and let it run through a cleaning cycle. Once the unit automatically shuts off, thoroughly rinse your denture.

Photo Credit Denture HyGenie 2018

5. You will then use your soft toothbrush and toothpaste to gently massage and clean your gum tissues. And gently scrub your denture, rinse for immediate wear.

Photo Credit Denture HyGenie 2018

*** Ideally, you should leave your denture in the unit overnight after running through the cleaning cycle to ensure that 99.9% of the odor-causing bacteria are killed and tough stains are removed. Always rinse thoroughly before replacing in your mouth. Your denture is now restored and refreshed.

***Take care of your DH Ultrasonic Unit so that it can take care of your denture. Simply unplug the unit, empty the water, rinse with fresh water and let dry after each use. Do NOT submerge your ultrasonic unit in water.

EXTRA CARE for a Removable Implant Denture

In the case of a removable implant denture, you can use the regular cleaning protocol above, with the exception of one area. It is very important that You also clean the implants in your mouth. You must remove the denture, clean thoroughly around the implants with a soft-bristle tooth brush (with a non-abrasive toothpaste, if it feels "sandy" do NOT use it) and/or a dental water irrigation device, such as a water flosser. Rinsing with an antiseptic mouthwash will also help keep your appliances and mouth clean and fresh. As with standard dentures, it is wise to remove them at night and sleep with them out of your mouth. It is also very important to make and keep dental hygiene appointments with your provider to maintain the health of the implants, just as you would for natural teeth.

EXTRA CARE for a Fixed Implant Denture & All-On-4

Fixed implant dentures and all-on-4 fixed "bridges" have a different cleaning protocol because they do not come out of your mouth to be cleaned, so you have to clean them inside of your mouth.

You first must brush your denture and oral tissues with a soft-bristled toothbrush. Next you should use a dental water irrigation device such as a water flosser, to clean around your implants under the denture/ bridge, clean the gums under the denture/ bridge and to clean the bottom side of the denture/bridge. You can also utilize a dental floss threader. Your dental provider can also provide you with micro-diameter cleaning utensils to properly clean under your fixed bridge. Rinsing with an antiseptic mouthwash throughout the day, will also help keep your appliances and mouth clean and fresh. It is also very important to make and keep dental hygiene appointments with your provider to maintain the health of the implants, just as you would for natural teeth.

Chapter 7

DENTURE MAINTENANCE
Living with Dentures

Photo Credit Shutterstock 1492368110

"I have my new smile...What could go wrong? What should I do about it?"

Daily:

When your dentures are not in your mouth, it is very important to keep them moist. You should clean them first and then you can put them in your denture cup, either in fresh water or in denture cleanser.

In addition to taking proper care of your denture, you still need to take care of your mouth. To do this, you should of course, brush and floss any natural teeth you have remaining. Taking very good care of the remaining natural teeth in your mouth will help your prosthetic last longer and keep your mouth healthy. In addition, you should use a soft bristle brush and gently brush your gums and tongue. This will not only clean your mouth, but will stimulate blood flow to reduce tissue resorption. It is recommended that you take out your dentures at bedtime to give the supporting bone structures in your mouth a break and to reduce bone resorption, which you would like to keep at a minimum because the bone is mostly what your denture is fitted to and helps to ensure a good fit of your denture.

Tip
Follow the previous Care section to maintain your specific type of denture.

Bi-Yearly or Yearly:

Depending on your provider's recommendation you should schedule an examination appointment with your dental provider either every 6 months or yearly. At this appointment they will evaluate the fit, function, appearance and condition of your denture. You will also receive an oral examination of your mouth's condition and get health screenings completed. At these appointments, you might be advised that you need to schedule a reline appointment to improve the fit of your denture or possibly other services, as needed. If you have a partial denture, you will get a full mouth tooth examination, including x-rays, in addition to a denture evaluation to ensure that the teeth that the partial denture are anchored to are still in adequate condition. You can also have your dentures professionally cleaned and polished to restore their condition.

As Needed:
Of course, there are going to be unforeseen issues that will come up between your daily care and your yearly examinations. You can always schedule an appointment with your provider if you have concerns regarding your mouth or your denture. The next section will review common problems and what you should do if something should come up. When in doubt, schedule an appointment with your provider. A quick, easy appointment could save you months of discomfort.

Photo Credit Shutterstock 277383077

Common Denture Problems

Your mouth is in a constant state of change. One day you might be dehydrated which causes your oral tissues shrink and your denture to be loose. Maybe you lost weight and now your denture is loose and causing sore spots? As well as the age-old, normal, problem of bone resorption, causing you to have loose dentures. What is resorption? Now that your jaw bones are subject to the chewing forces placed on them from the denture, they gradually break down and leave you with a loose denture, which leads to sore spots. All of these problems are normal. Do not be concerned, there are ways to remedy almost every denture problem.

My denture is loose?
Your mouth is in a state of constant change. The tissues are changing with time and the jaw bones shrink. Other factors such as being dehydrated, certain

medications and weight loss can affect the fit of your denture. As long as the denture is in good condition, your dental provider will most likely recommend a denture reline. A denture reline will refit the denture to the current oral situation. If the denture is in poor condition, your dental provider will most likely recommend you have a new denture made that will not only fit properly, but allow it to function effectively.

My mouth is sore everywhere?
Do not attempt to adjust your denture yourself. You can cause serious damage to your denture that will require additional professional services to obtain a good denture fit. The best option is to contact your dental provider and schedule an appointment for them to evaluate the situation. As I have mentioned previously, your mouth is always changing, so occasionally you will need to have your dentures adjusted, a temporary tissue conditioning liner placed or a reline completed to make your denture fit comfortably. In the meantime, take your denture out and several times a day to help heal the sore area. If you cannot take the denture out due to work or other reasons, you can pick up numbing gels from the pharmacy to help get you by until you see your dental provider.

I have one spot that hurts really bad and looks like a canker sore?
This is typically called a denture sore or denture ulcer. Your denture is most likely rubbing on that particular area and will need to be adjusted by your dental provider. Do not attempt to adjust the denture yourself. You can cause serious damage to your denture that will require additional professional services to obtain a good denture fit. The best option is to contact your dental provider and schedule an appointment for them to remedy the situation. As I have mentioned previously, your mouth is always changing, so occasionally you will need to have your dentures adjusted, a temporary tissue conditioning liner placed or a reline completed to make your denture fit comfortably. In the meantime, take your denture out and rinse your mouth with warm salt water or an antiseptic mouthwash several times a day to help heal the irritated area. If you cannot take the denture out due to work or other reasons, you can pick up numbing gels from the pharmacy to help get you by until you see your dental provider.

My chin is starting to move forward and stick out, what is going on?
This is usually due to denture tooth wear and your lower jaw is coming too far forward. You should make an appointment with your dental to provider to see

what can be done either to improve your current denture or to replace it.

I can't speak very well?
If you are new to the denture world, this could just be a matter of getting used to speaking with a denture in your mouth. I often suggest that people talk as much as possible or read aloud until their mouth becomes accustomed to speaking with a denture in place. If after time, you still feel that you are struggling with this problem, schedule an appointment with your dental provider. There are several ways that they can assist with your speech if it continues to be a problem.

I am gagging on my upper denture?
If you are new to the denture world, this could just be a matter of getting used to having a denture in your mouth. I often suggest that people focus on breathing though their noses until they become accustomed to having a denture in their mouth. It is very helpful to take slow, deep breaths through your nose if you feel like you may gag. If after time, you still feel that you are struggling with this problem, schedule an appointment with your dental provider. There are several ways that they can assist if it continues to be a problem.

Why doesn't the lower stay in as well as the upper?
Your upper denture will normally suction to the roof of your mouth, while the lower denture basically "floats" on the mandibular jaw bone. If your jaw bone anatomy is large and robust, you will have fewer problems with this. If your lower jaw bone seems very flat and does not have a good "ridge", you will struggle with this more. I would suggest you first try denture adhesive. If this does not work adequately, you should schedule an appointment with your dental provider. Sometimes they can adjust the denture to help with this problem, some providers offer soft relines on the lower denture, or they may advise you to consider implant treatments.

I have a white, yeasty coating in my mouth?
You may have a case of Oral Candidiasis. This a medical condition of the mouth, also known as oral thrush. A yeast/fungal infection of the mucous membranes in your mouth. It can cause a burning sensation, metallic or salty tastes, and white spots in the mouth. Generally treated with antifungal drugs. You should schedule an appointment with your dental provider to have them complete an exam and get you medication, if needed.

Why are the corners of my mouth cracking and crusty?

You may have Angular Cheilitis. This is an inflammation of one or both corners of the mouth. Often this is itchy, painful, red and can be crusty. This is usually due to denture tooth wear in an older denture. If you have a newer denture, it may not be "tall" enough and this causes your mouth to overclose, creating this inflammation. You should make an appointment with your dental to provider to see what can be done either to improve your current denture or to have it replaced.

My denture tooth broke out?

First things first. Did you lose the tooth or do you still have it? If you still have it, you should save it and take it to your denture professional with your denture. Sometimes they can re-attach the tooth rather than having to use a new tooth. This can usually save you a little bit of money as well. <u>Do NOT use superglue!!</u> This creates a mess for the dental laboratory technician and often times they cannot re-use the tooth. In certain situations, the lab technician will not be able to re-use the tooth.

If you do NOT have the tooth that has come out of your denture, do not fear, the dental laboratory stocks all shapes, sizes and colors of denture teeth and with replace the tooth in your denture to match the rest of your teeth.

My denture tooth chipped?
Depending on the severity of the chip, sometimes your dental professional can buff out the chip. If the chip is more significant, then generally, the dental professional will have the denture tooth replaced with a matching tooth.

I lost weight and now my denture doesn't fit?
Your mouth is in a state of constant change. The tissues are changing with time and the jaw bones shrink. Other factors such as being dehydrated, certain medications and weight loss can affect the fit of your denture. As long as the denture is in good condition, your dental provider will most likely recommend a denture reline. A denture reline will refit the denture to the current tissue situation. If the denture is in poor condition, your dental provider will most likely recommend you have a new denture made that will not only fit properly, but allow it to function effectively.

My denture broke on the pink acrylic?
Don't worry, this happens sometimes the denture or bit into something too hard, sometimes the acrylic can break. It is after all, just plastic. Do NOT attempt to repair it yourself, as you can destroy the fit of your denture and it will not fit properly again without additional professional services. <u>Do NOT use superglue!!</u> This creates a mess for the dental

laboratory technician and often times they cannot accurately place broken pieces of your denture back together, leading to an ill-fitting denture. What you should do, is contact your dental provider immediately and they will repair the acrylic properly. Depending on the location of the crack/break, your dental provider may have to reinforce the area with metal. Usually a denture is repair is not terribly expensive or time consuming, especially compared to replacing the denture. In fact, some clinics, depending on their dental facility, can repair the denture within the day.

My dog chewed on my denture...Help?
Dogs LOVE dentures!! Make sure to keep your dentures securely away from pets. But in case it does happen, do NOT attempt to repair it yourself, as you can destroy the fit of your denture and it will not fit properly again without additional professional services. What you should do, is contact your dental provider immediately and they will determine if they can repair the acrylic properly. Depending on the severity of the damage, your dental provider may or may not be able to repair the denture.

Is my denture growing mold?
The simple answer is, it could be. If you are storing it in water for extended periods of time and not changing the water, this can be a happy growing ground for bacteria and molds.

How do I store my denture for an extended time period?

If you have a spare denture and would like to store it until it is needed, you need to be very diligent in the care of the stored denture. You will have to ensure that you first of all adequately clean and disinfect the denture. Then you will place in a plain water solution and will still have to clean it at minimum, every couple of days to avoid severe bacteria and mold issues.

How Long Will My Dentures Last?

Shutterstock Photo Credit 497004073

The replacement of your denture is to ensure proper fit, function, aesthetics and to maintain hygiene. Even if you think that the denture is working great, it is still best to have a professional analyze it for the proper fit, tooth wear, and of course, aesthetics. Denture acrylic is porous and, therefore, it can harbor bacteria and stains. It is best for your overall health to follow the replacement timeline guidelines to ensure that your smile stays as functional and healthy as possible.

All of the below are simply time <u>guidelines</u>, but everyone is an individual, with individual needs and situations. If you are diligent about the maintenance of your prosthesis and mouth, your prosthesis can last a very long time. On the other hand, your prosthesis endures significant stresses and "lives" in a warm, moist environment, which makes it prone to bacteria growth. In addition, even with the greatest care, dentures wear out and the materials used to make dentures will need to be replaced eventually. There is no substitution for being confident in your smile and the freshness of your breath. It is very important to replace and rejuvenate your smile as often as you see fit and live your life with a fresh, beautiful smile.

Flipper- Suggested replacement is "as soon as possible". Flippers are generally used as a transition denture. Meaning that you are expected to lose additional teeth and the flipper is maintaining your smile and/or dental function until the teeth fail or are extracted, at which point, you would get a more permanent RPD, such as a flexible RPD or a cast metal RPD. A flipper can also be used as a temporary device to maintain your smile until you get a more permanent solution of a bridge or implant if additional teeth are not anticipated to fail.

Acrylic or Interim RPD- Suggested replacement is "as soon as possible". Acrylic partials are generally used as a transition denture. Meaning that you are expected to lose additional teeth and the acrylic partial is maintaining your smile and/or dental function until the teeth fail or are extracted, at which point, you would get a more permanent RPD, such as a flexible RPD or a cast metal RPD.

Flexible RPD- Suggested replacement is on average every 5 years, if you do not lose any additional teeth. The replacement of your denture is to ensure proper fit, function, aesthetics and to maintain hygiene.

Cast metal RPD-Suggested replacement is on average every 5 -7 years, if you do not lose any additional teeth. The replacement of your denture is to ensure proper fit, function, aesthetics and to maintain hygiene.

Complete Denture- Suggested replacement is on average of 5-10 years. The replacement of your denture is to ensure proper fit, function, aesthetics and to maintain hygiene.

Immediate Denture-Suggested replacement is within first year after your extractions are completed, your mouth has healed, and the best option is to transition to a complete denture for better fit, function, and appearance. Suggested replacement is on average of 5-10 years.
If you and your provider are satisfied with your initial temporary immediate denture, with proper care and maintenance it can last 2-5 years.

Implant Denture (Fixed or Removable)- Regularly scheduled dental appointments with dental provider will ensure that your mouth is healthy, and that your denture is fitting properly. Your provider will take occasional x-rays to verify that your implants are healthy and still in the proper position for ideal function. The attachments, retention rings and clips wear out fairly frequently and usually are replaced once or twice a year. Suggested denture replacement is on average 5-10 years. Your implants will not need replaced, unless one fails. The replacement denture will be made to use your existing healthy implants.

All-On-4-Typically you will get a temporary acrylic fixed dental "bridge" that is meant to last only through your healing process. At the time that your dental provider determines that your mouth is adequately healed and that your implants are integrated (healed/secure), you will then convert your acrylic dental appliance to a more permanent fixed dental "bridge". This will be your more permanent restoration, dental "bridge". Regularly scheduled dental appointments with your dental provider will ensure that your mouth is healthy, and that your denture is fitting properly. Your provider will take occasional x-rays to verify that your implants are healthy and still in the proper position for ideal function. The attachments, retention rings and clips wear out fairly frequently and usually are replaced once or twice a year.

Chapter 8

CONCLUSION

Shutterstock Photo Credit 492354154

"I can eat, talk and smile with confidence!"

Losing teeth is a normal part of life and a person's smile is usually one of the first things that others will notice. Dentures and implants are a great solution to keep you confidently smiling and healthy. Without a healthy dental situation, it is difficult for you to eat a variety of nutritious foods, which then ultimately inhibits your well-being. I hope that this guide has answered most of your questions and informed you on the numerous options you have for natural tooth replacement. I also hope that this guide has helped ease your nervousness about how to take care of your mouth and dentures, once you have gotten your new smile. Most of all, I hope I have given you peace of mind, in that dentures are not a negative thing that happens to you in life, but something that can actually improve the quality of your life. Dentures can open your eyes to a whole new life. They can increase your self-esteem, allow you to eat foods you have not enjoyed in years, and allow you to enjoy activities you love in a pain-free, confident manner.

We only get one life, why not choose to lead it SMILING?

www.ingramcontent.com/pod-product-compliance
Lightning Source LLC
Chambersburg PA
CBHW021114080526
44587CB00010B/510